WOWIE ZOWIE!
Thirty Years of Rock'N'Roll Trivia

is packed with all the facts that the casual fan or serious aficionado could ever want to know about the music called rock'n'roll. More than another encyclopedia, it's a fascinating pastiche, a rock around the time clock, spanning three decades worth of colorful pop memorabilia. By the way, the answers to those cover questions are:
1. Country Joe and the Fish 2. Ray Davies 3. Mrs. Dick Clark 4. Alvin and the Chipmunks 5. B.B. King 6. Dick Dodd 7. Procul Harem 8. Elvis Costello 9. Ringo Starr 10. Tony Orlando

*TQ—Your Trivia Quotient—is scored this way:

10 right—Yeh Yeh!
7 to 9—Papa-Oom-Mow-Mow!
5 to 6—Wooly Booly.
4 or less—Boo Hoo. Get with it!

It's time to read . . .

ROCK'N'ROLL TRIVIA

Other Works by Fred L. Worth

The Trivia Encyclopedia
*Super Trivia**
Country Western Quiz Book
*Hollywood Trivia (with David Strauss)***
Heroes and Superheroes Trivia Quiz Book
The Great Movie Quiz Library Series
The Elvis Companion (with Steve Tamerius)
*Super Trivia II***

*Published by
WARNER BOOKS

**To be published by
WARNER BOOKS

THIRTY YEARS OF ROCK 'N' ROLL TRIVIA

by Fred L. Worth

A Warner Communications Company

WARNER BOOKS EDITION

Cover design by New Studio, Inc.

Warner Books, Inc., 75 Rockefeller Plaza, New York, N.Y. 10019

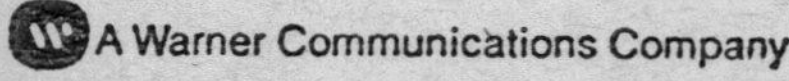

Printed in the United States of America

First Printing: September, 1980

10 9 8 7 6 5 4 3 2

Acknowledgments

I would like to thank the talents of Susan Worth, Steve Tamerius, Gary Owens, Dane Pascoe, Tom Kirby, Don Fink, Bonnie Redelings, Vince Rolfe and David Glagovsky for their help in making this fifteen-year dream possible.

Special thanks to Ken Anthony, a promising young announcer of KLIV AM (San Jose, California). With Ken's talents, he has a super career ahead.

Author's Note

The author has every intention of updating this encyclopedia work in the future with new and corrected material. If you, the reader, wish to add to or correct any existing information (unless it has already been submitted), the author will acknowledge your assistance in the next edition.

The Rock 'n' Roll school in general concentrated on a minimum of melodic line and a maximum of rhythmic noise, deliberately competing with the artistic ideals of the jungle itself.

—*Encyclopedia Britannica Yearbook (1955)*

Characteristics: an unrelenting, socking syncopation that sounds like a bullwhip; a choleric saxophone honking mating call sounds; an electric guitar turned up so loud that its sound shatters and splits; a vocal group that shudders and exercises violently to the beat while roughly chanting either a near-nonsense phrase or a moronic lyric in hillbilly idiom.

—*Time Magazine (1956)*

Rock and roll is phony and false, and sung, written and played for the most part by cretinous goons.

—*Frank Sinatra* (1957)*

*In 1974 Frank Sinatra would record *Bad Bad Leroy Brown*

Rock 'N' Roll—The Beginning

Alan Freed is often credited with coining the phrase "rock 'n' roll," yet in nineteen forty-eight a group called Billy Mathews and the Balladeers recorded a record titled *Rock and Roll,* and one year earlier in 1947 Wild Bill Moore recorded *We're Gonna Roll.* We can even go back earlier to the 1934 movie *Transatlantic Merry-Go-Round,* where the Boswell sisters sang a tune called *Rock and Roll.* But many, including myself, believe that the Fats Domino instrumental *The Fat Man,* recorded on December 10, 1949, was one of the first rock 'n' roll tunes, although traces of the music can be heard earlier. But one has to begin somewhere, and 1949 was the year—thirty-one years ago.

Though Alan Freed surely didn't coin the phrase, he did apply it to the music that became a blend of rhythm and blues, gospel, and country music; and that wonderful sound is still called rock 'n' roll thirty years after its introduction.

In this book the most common background knowledge of each performer is intentionally omitted, since this is not intended as a history or a biography of rock 'n' roll stars. There already exist numerous books on the subject, and such information can be found in so many other works that most music buffs have already read the same story dozens of times. The information in this book is of an esoteric nature. Not all artists and groups are present, but their inclusion will surely come with time and an updated edition of *Thirty Years of Rock 'n' Roll Trivia.*

Fred L. Worth

Preface
by Gary Owens

Needless to say, I was very pleased that "Mr. Trivia," Fred L. Worth, should ask me to write actual words for the introduction of this magic volume, *Thirty Years of Rock 'n' Roll Trivia.*

The "Gary Owens Show" started in radio and television almost concomitantly with the birth of rock and roll, and it was an electrifying time, as we look back on that important part of pop culture. This book is a reflection of those times, not always through a Fellini-like lens, gauging the move from our cartoon existence in the fifties to our loss of innocence in the sixties.

For many years, I performed as a rock and roll deejay. (I still hate the term *deejay!* It sounds like something that should have been ripped soundly from an anthropologist's notebook in the late 1940s.) Over the span of years, I've been fortunate in being able to work with all of the greats—either in radio since I was sixteen, or in TV since I was eighteen (over 10,000 radio shows and some 600 network television shows).

My first gig was at KOIL in Omaha in the mid-50s. I was doubly impressed by the artists I played on the air, and met and enjoyed off the air. (During those years, I was so broke, an orphan in Korea supported *me.*)

Those were the days of mucho dance hops, grinding

our vertebrae and undulating in motion with our small universe. (Considering my shoddy dancing ability, it was more like flopping around with a wounded octopus!) I could have been a better dancer, but my knees kept vapor-locking!

In retrospect, Omaha, Nebraska, seems an unusual place for the birth of rock and roll radio! Todd Storz was the first to set up an entire radio station that played *only* hits. Todd was on leave from the Navy, and while he sat in a small cafe, he noticed people shuffling in and playing the same records with recidivism on the friendly neighborhood jukebox. (When I was studying psychology, we had a *Kalikak* Box!) Cogently, young Mr. Storz made a chart of those records and their frequency of being played, thereby devising the format for the "top twenty" or "top forty" radio stations that suddenly sprang up around the nation. About the same time, another genius, Gordon McLendon (the young Old Scotsman), was doing almost the same thing in Dallas at KLIF, but putting more emphasis on the personality of his performers, to balance the hit music.

Storz, incidentally, died at the age of thirty-nine in the 1960s, a tragically young age for a man who had contributed so much to radio.

Fred Worth in this book has put forth many hours toil and expository diligence. He brings us the hard-core memorabilia, coupled with fascinating tangential excursions that make reliving that era even more fun than living it was!

He covers all the great pop and rock 'n' roll artists over the thirty-year span when radio and television stations were such an integral part in what was a phantasmagoric time for all of us.

It is interesting to note that music, like radio and TV,

is a situation of survival being a "sustained achievement." How many of the great artists from that period are still active and solvent today? One rock star whom I saw recently had aged considerably. We had last seen her in the late 1950s: she was now completely gray, except for her hair—which was orange!

There are so many fond memories that pop into my gnarled gourd, as time proves again that most of us are willing victims of W.P.A. (Wonderful Prolonged Adolescence). But it's wise to recall the apothegm, "The older a man gets, the better he could swim as a boy!"

Let me just give you some free association . . .

The Strawberry Alarm Clock . . . They were featured on our first TV series, Rowan and Martin's "Laugh In."

Diana Ross and the Supremes . . . I did several TV specials with them and *The Temptations* for NBC-TV, and took part in Diana's first acting bit. Dinah Shore had a beautiful special called "LIKE HEP!" *Lucille Ball, Rowan and Martin,* and *Dinah* were featured in a satire on *Snow White and the Seven Dwarfs.* And guess who played Snow White? That's right, it was lovely DIANA.

Remember the girl who teased, "Kookie, Kookie, Lend me your comb"? You know it was *Connie Stevens,* who was under contract to Warner Brothers at the same time *Edd Byrnes* was. Connie and I have been friends since 1959, when I cut my first record, Steve Allen's composition, "What Is A Freem." With the talented concert pianist George Greeley.

Elvis was indeed the King, no one will argue that fact. I first met him while nurgling at WNOE, New Orleans. His impact hit the area of the Vieux Carre the same way it hit Madison Avenue and Sunset Boulevard—with the power of a ramjet! It was the first time the staid St. Charles Hotel, just off Canal Street, had its giant doors flung open as hundreds of frenzied teenagers scampered through to grab and claw at Elvis's clothing and hair. (Plus his clothing that was made of hair.) I spoke with Elvis on later occasions in Hollywood and was always impressed with his quiet, polite manner.

Incidentally, at most radio stations in those halcyon days, *solid friendship* was usually when two DJs were mad at the same executive!

I was at KFWB in Hollywood, the top hit-making radio station in the world in the late 50s and early 60s. Each morning following my 6:00-9:00 A.M. show, I would stomp down the stairs to a cafe called Aldo's with many of my record promoter friends and just talk about the biz. Among the promo folk was a young man named Sonny Bono. One morning Sonny was sitting next to a cute slender young girl of sixteen named Cher Sarkisian. Well, if you are a pop history fan, you know what happened. They put together an act first known as Caesar and Cleo, and then were transmographied as SONNY AND CHER.

Herb Alpert and *Jerry Moss* have been longtime pals in this wonderful world. Herb started singing under the name of Dore Alpert, and he and Jerry (a much-loved record promoter) cut the *"Lonely Bull"* in a garage for about $600. Alpert and Moss then founded A and M Records. (Incidentally, after being founded, it has never been losted!) They both became multimillionaires in their first year.

There are so many anecdotes to share and so many people to mention, there isn't space to list them here, but I assure you there are so many funky tidbits in Fred's new book, that your memory banks will salivate all the way to the past. . . .

The Beach Boys started out as Kenny and the Cadets . . . remember in the early 60s when they influenced so many kids to cross America by surfboard? *Jan and Dean* . . . *Tony Orlando.* Tony was originally a demo singer for Don Kirshner . . . *Bobby Rydell,* another great singer from South Philly . . . I recall *Fats Domino* in New Orleans. Fats owned more than 300 pairs of shoes at one time! . . . *Pat Boone.* Yes, Pat is a direct descendant of Daniel Boone. *Roy Orbison:* Roy was influenced by Pat to grab at a singing career and go for the big time. . . . Memories of *Paul* and *Linda McCartney's* private party onboard the Queen Mary in Long Beach. I realized when I got up on stage to say some nice things about Paul and Linda that I was wearing one black sock and one brown sock! . . . *Johnny Mathis:* Johnny lives in a house in Hollywood once owned by Howard Hughes for his many rendezvous with Jean Harlow—it has a secret tunnel in the wine cellar. . . .

Buddy Holly: I knew Buddy when he was just getting started with his recordings. The last name was originally spelled H-O-L-L-E-Y. *Freddy Cannon* . . . *Gene McDaniels* . . . *Brenda Lee* . . . *James Darren* . . . I remember *George Harrison* sitting with Eric Idle and Terry Gilliam of Monty Python's Flying Circus at a funny table chortling (a word created by Lewis Carroll, incidentally). George is the big financial backer for the Python films. . . . *Tommy Sands* . . . *Nancy Sinatra* . . . *Jimmie Rodgers*

. . . *Skip and Flip* (who were *Clyde Batton* and *Gary Paxton*. Gary later went on to "Alley Oop" fame with the Hollywood Argyles. . . .

Paul Anka . . . Snuff Garrett . . . Jimmy Bowen . . . Jerry Lee Lewis: Jerry was married three times by the age of twenty-two. . . . *The Everly Brothers . . . Nino and April . . . Johnny and Dorsey Burnette* (both gone now) . . . *Ray Stevens:* Ray was once a deejay in Albany, Georgia. . . . *Neil Sedaka . . . Bobby Vee . . . Jackie DeShannon . . . Glen Campbell:* Glen is the only celeb in the music biz who comes from a home town that's even smaller than mine in South Dakota. My village boasts a population of 600. Glen's hometown of Delight, Arkansas, has 200. When he was going to school back there, he used to drive a sports model tractor with white sidewall lugs!

Sam Cooke . . . Jerry Butler . . . Ernie Freeman . . . Connie Francis: Connie once told me she had played accordian since the age of four! . . . *Johnny Rivers . . . Paul Revere and the Raiders . . . The Hilltoppers . . . Bobby Darin;* Bobby said that "Splish Splash" took less than two minutes to compose. . . .

Joe Seracino and the Mar-Kets . . . Chris Montez . . . Carol Connors and the Teddy Bears . . . Johnny Tillotson: Johnny has the biggest collection of memorabilia from radio shows—like the old Lone Ranger Rings, etc. . . . *The Champs . . . Phil Spector . . . Bobby Freeman:* Used to do many dance hops with Bobby in the San Francisco area. . . . *Frankie Avalon . . . Annette . . . Fabian . . . Rod Lauren . . . Ricky Nelson:* Ricky imitated Elvis on an "Ozzie and Harriet" TV show, and that gave him his send-off as a singer. . . . *Gary Usher . . . The Monkees . . .*

How can I possibly mention so many great stars that I've been lucky enough to work with? Your best bet is to read this volume of Fred Worth's—and read it carefully. Fred has carefully detailed INSIDE information on which stars today are making a living selling medicated leotards to aging ballerinas, which ones are card-carrying crop dusters, and which ones are naughty and nice! Summing it up, I think we should all remember the words of Gayla Peevey . . . and I'm sure we all will.

Best Krelbs and happy trivia

from Gary Owens
Supreme High Nurgle, Sunset Boulevard

KMPC
Hollywood, California

A

A Lovers Concerto

The Toys' 1965 hit *A Lovers Concerto* was based on Johann Sebastian Bach's *Minuet in G.*

A & M Records

Herb Alpert's A & M Records complex was built in 1966 on the site of the old Charlie Chaplin movie studio in Hollywood.

A Night With Daddy G

In 1961 the Church Street Five recorded a minor instrumental hit titled *A Night With Daddy G.* Later that same year Gary "U.S." Bonds added lyrics to the music, and the hit *Quarter To Three* was born.

A Star Is Born

Priscilla, the sister of Rita Coolidge (wife of Kris Kristofferson), is married to organist Booker T. Jones. Rita, Kris, and Booker, all appeared in the 1976 movie *A Star Is Born.*

A Whiter Shade of Pale

Procol Harum's 1967 hit *A Whiter Shade of Pale* was based on Johann Sebastian Bach's cantata *Sleepers Awake.*

Abba

Abba, the most popular group in the world in 1977, has a palindrome for a name. The group's name was actually adapted from the first letters of the group's members: *A*gatha Ulvaeus, *B*jorn Ulvaeus, *B*enny Andersson, *A*nnifrid Andersson.

When Abba first began singing English lyrics, they had to learn the words phonetically since none of them spoke English.

As of 1978 the group became the largest grossing export of Sweden. Volvo was number two.

Abbott Records

Jim Reeves, the Browns, and Floyd Cramer, all recorded on the Abbott Record label out of Shreveport prior to becoming artists for RCA Victor Records.

Abbreviations

O.C. Smith	Ocie Smith
B.J. Thomas	Billy Joe Thomas
B.T. Express	Brothers Trucking Express
M.G.'s	Memphis Group
MFSB	Mothers–Fathers–Sisters–Brothers
E.L.O.	Electric Light Orchestra

Lou Adler

Record producer Lou Adler was once the victim of a kidnapping.

Ain't It A Shame

In 1956 when Pat Boone covered Fats Domino's recording of *Ain't It A Shame,* the title was changed to *Ain't That A Shame* (supposedly a grammatical correction). Ironically, on United Artists' Legendary Masters Series the Fats Domino double album lists the song as *Ain't That A Shame,* rather than by the original title.

Ain't No Sunshine

On Bill Wither's best-selling record, *Ain't No Sunshine,* recorded in 1971, Stephen Stills played lead guitar.

Alfie

Although *Alfie* became a superhit for Dionne Warwick, a little-known fact is that in the 1966 movie *Alfie,* it was Cher who sang the movie's theme song.

Muhammad Ali

In 1964 heavyweight boxing champion Muhammad Ali had a minor hit with the Ben E. King classic *Stand By Me,* with *I am the Greatest* as the flip side.

All American Boy

The early 1959 hit *All American Boy* was credited to Bill Parsons because the producers for Fraternity Records mixed up the two names of a pair of young singers who recorded several demos. The voice on the song is actually that of Bobby Bare, who has never been credited for his own recording. It is the voice on the flip-side song *Rubber Dolly* that belongs to Bill Parsons.

All Stars

Several members of Junior Walker's band the All Stars are prior members of Al Green's group the Creations.

All You Need Is Love

Mick Jagger, Graham Nash, Keith Moon, Keith Richard, Marianne Faithful, Garry Leeds, Jane Asher, and Patti Boyd, along with John, Paul, George, and Ringo sang chorus on the Beatles' song *All You Need is Love.*

Lee Allen

Lee Allen, who in 1957 had one hit record with *Walkin' With Mr. Lee,* is the sax player lead on many of the hit records of Fats Domino and Little Richard.

Rick Allen

Rick Allen was a member of the Gentrys when they reached the top ten in 1965 with *Keep On Dancing* and later with the Box Tops when they charted *The Letter* (1967) and *Cry Like A Baby* (1968).

Arvee Allens

Arvee Allens, who once had a single released in 1959 titled *Fast Freight*, was actually Ritchie Valens recording under a pseudonym.

Duane Allman

Before forming the Allman Brothers with brother Greg, Duane Allman was a studio musician who backed such musicians as Aretha Franklin and Wilson Pickett.

Duane Allman and Berry Oakley

Tragedy has hit rock'n' roll time and time again. But one of the most tragic incidents was the death of Duane Allman and Berry Oakley, members of the Allman Brothers Band. The musicians were killed on motorcycles a year apart, Duane Allman on October 29, 1971, Berry Oakley on November 11, 1972, both near the same location in Macon, Georgia.

Allman Brothers

Duane and Greg Allman once sang under the name the Allman Joys.

Tommy Allsup

Cricket member Tommy Allsup gave up his seat to Ritchie Valens on the tragic plane flight that resulted in the death of Valens, Buddy Holly, and J.P. Richardson February 3, 1959. Likewise, another member of the Crickets, Waylon Jennings, relinquished his seat to Richardson after having lost a flip of a coin.

Herb Alpert

If you believe that Herb Alpert is of latin descent, consider this: his mother was born in Hungary, his father in Russia.

Prior to recording his first record *The Lonely Bull,* Herb Alpert was one of the drum players in Cecil B. DeMille's 1956 version of *The Ten Commandments.* He appeared in the scene where Moses is descending from the mountain, his back to the audience while he beats on a drum.

Herb Alpert was one of the co-writers of Sam Cooke's 1960 hit *Wonderful World.*

Lani Alpert, the wife of millionaire Herb Alpert, was once a vocalist with Sergio Mendez and Brazil '66.

America

(Gerry Beckley, Dewey Bunnell, Dan Peck.) All of the album releases of America begin with the letter "H" with the exception of their debut album *America,* which is commonly referred to as their *Horse with No Name* LP, named after the number-one hit from that album in 1972. The albums are: *America* (1972), *Holiday* (1974), *Harbour* (1977), *Homecoming* (1972), *Hearts* (1975), *History—America's Greatest Hits* (1975), *Hat Trick* (1973), *Hideaway* (1976).

The Americans

The Americans was a tribute record about the charity of the American people recorded in 1974 by Canadian Byron MacGregor. It reached #4 in the top 100.

Anatomy

Group names that are part of the anatomy:

Heart
Toe Fat
Head, Hands and Feet
Butts Band
Arm and Hammer
Horselips
Badfinger

And I Love Her So

The beautiful ballad *And I Love Her So,* made popular by crooner Perry Como (his fifteenth gold record), was composed by Don McLean.

Peter Anders and Vincent Poncia

Singers Peter Anders and Vincent Poncia have been the voices for the studio groups the Tradewinds, and the Innocence and were previously members of the early 1960s group the Videls whose biggest hit was *Mr. Lonely.*

Lynn Anderson

Many rock 'n' roll and country singers have had varied backgrounds prior to becoming stars. Lynn Anderson, for example, who hit the charts in 1970 with her version of the Joe South song *Rose Garden,* had previously been a member of Lawrence Welk's television show.

Paul Anka

In Fisher Park High in Hull, Quebec, Paul Anka sang with a group called the Bobby Soxers.

Paul Anka, with the assistance of Johnny Carson, composed *Here's Johnny,* "The Tonight Show" theme song. For this one composition, Paul Anka receives $30,000 a year.

Anna Records

Anna Records is a Detroit record label founded by Anna Gordy, sister of Berry Gordy, Jr. Anna actually established her label prior to Berry founding Tamla Records. The biggest hit on Anna was Barrett Strong's 1960 hit *Money.* Singer Marvin Gaye was once married to Anna Gordy.

Ape Call

On Nervous Norvus' 1956 recording of *Ape Call,* it was radio comedian Red Blanchard who supplied the ape calls in the background.

The Archies

In 1969 the obscure group the Archies had the number-one hit song of the year with *Sugar Sugar.* The Archies were musicians for the television cartoon series *Archie.* The musician's real names were never released.

Arista Records

Arista Records, the home label of Barry Manilow, the Bay City Rollers, Tony Orlando, and others, was founded in 1974 by Clive Davis only after he had been fired from his position as president of Columbia Records.

Joan Armatrading

Singer/songwriter Joan Armatrading was once an actress who appeared in a stage version of *Hair*.

Peter Asher

Linda Ronstadt and James Taylor's manager, Peter Asher, was once half of the duet of Peter & Gordon, whose biggest hit, *A World Without Love,* was written by John Lennon and Paul McCartney. Paul McCartney met Peter while dating his sister Jane Asher.

Rolling Stone Magizine voted Peter Asher "Producer off the Year" for 1977.

Ashford and Simpson

Before Nick Ashford and Valerie Simpson became a strong singing duo, the pair wrote such classics as *You're All I Need To Get By* and *Ain't No Mountain High Enough.*

The Association

The Association provided the musical background for the 1969 movie *Goodbye Columbus.*

Terry Kirkman, a former member of the Association and composer of the songs *Cherish* and *Windy,* is today a writer for the television game show "Name That Tune."

Assumed Names Used by Artists

The following artists have made records under the following assumed or original names:

Allman Joys	Allman Brothers
Arvie Allens	Ritchie Valens
Vance Arnold	Joe Cocker
Del Ashley	David Gates
Baby Ray and the Ferns	Frank Zappa
Bad Habbits	Delaney and Bonnie
Beach Bums	Bob Seger
Beat Brothers	Beatles
Beefeaters	Byrds
Caesar and Cleo	Sonny and Cher
Campers	Crickets
Centuries	Buckinghams
Choir	Raspberries
Don Christy	Sonny Bono
Craftsmen	Johnny and the Hurricanes
Crossfires	Turtles
Bertell Dache	Tony Orlando
Jimmy Dale	Jimmy Clanton
Darrel and the Oxfords	Tokens
Terry Day	Terry Melcher
Jackie Dee	Jackie DeShannon
Johnny Dee	John D. Loudermilk
Dialtones	Randy and the Rainbows
Eastmen	Del Vikings
Ebe Sneezer and the Epidemics	John D. Loudermilk
Eddie and the Evergreens	Sha Na Na
Falling Pebbles	Buckinghams
Felix and the Escorts	Young Rascals

Four Lovers	Four Seasons
Four Pennies	Chiffons
Four Winds	Tokens
Artie Garr	Art Garfunkel
Gary and Clyde	Skip and Flip
Gary and the Nite Lites	American Breed
Golliwogs	Creedence Clearwater Revival
Bob Guy	Frank Zappa
Harbor Lights	Jay and the Americans
The Hawk	Jerry Lee Lewis
High Numbers	Who
Intervals	Fifth Dimension
Python Lee Jackson	Rod Stewart
Paul Kane	Paul Simon
Kenny and the Cadets	Beach Boys
King Lizard	Kim Fowley
Jerry Landis	Paul Simon
Larry and the Legends	Four Seasons
Levon and the Hawks	The Band
Magic Touch	Vito and the Salutations
Marksman	Ventures
Bonnie Jo Mason	Cher
Bob McFadden	Rod McKuen
Gary Michaels	Mickey Gilley
Newporters	Walker Brothers
Other Tikis	Harper's Bizarre
Paramours	Righteous Brothers
Primettes	Supremes
Icky Remut	Ike Turner
Rick and the Raiders	McCoys
Eddie Robbins	Frankie Lymon
Rockaways	Jay and the Americans

Kenneth Rogers	Kenny Rogers
Ronnie and the Relatives	Ronettes
Neil Scott	Neil Bogart
Jackie Shannon	Jackie DeShannon
Bobby Sheridan	Charlie Rich
Billy Shields	Tony Orlando
Ronny Sommers	Sonny Bono
Sir Chauncey	Ernie Freeman
Survivors	Beach Boys
Suzy and the Red Stripes	Linda McCartney
T-Bones	Hamilton, Joe Frank and Reynolds
Trade Winds	Videls
True Taylor	Paul Simon
Scotty Wayne	Freddie Fender
Sonny Wilson	Conway Twitty
Veronica	Ronnie Spector
Donny Young	Johnny Paycheck

At The Hop

Danny and the Juniors' 1957 hit *At The Hop* was originally titled *Do The Bop,* but at the suggestion of Dick Clark the title was changed to *At The Hop.*

The Atlanta Rhythm Section

The Atlanta Rhythm Section is the uncredited group that provides the theme music for "ABCs Wide World of Sports" television series.

Guitarist Barry Bailey, bassist Paul Goddard, drummer Robert Nix, and keyboard man Dean Daughtry of the Atlanta Rhythm Section, all formerly toured with Roy Orbison as members of the Candymen. Producer Buddy Buie and guitarist J.R. Cobb of the Atlanta Rhythm Section wrote the top 10 hits *Spooky* and *Stormy* in 1968 while members of the Classics IV.

Attitude Dancing

On Carly Simon's *Attitude Dancing,* Carole King is one of the background vocalists.

Au Go Go Singers

Richie Furay and Steve Stills were both members of the obscure group Au Go Go Singers

Frankie Avalon

Prior to becoming a teenage vocalist, Frankie Avalon appeared on several different television shows hosted by Jackie Gleason, Paul Whiteman, and Ray Anthony. On the shows Frankie played trumpet.

Hoyt Axton

Hoyt Axton's mother Mae Axton is the co-writer of Elvis Presley's 1956 first million-seller, *Heartbreak Hotel.* She is the sister of David Boren, one-time governor of Oklahoma.

Diana Ayoub

The girl who in 1957 inspired Paul Anka to compose his biggest selling record *Diana* was Diana Ayoub, his baby-sitter.

B

Baby Sittin' Boogie

In 1960 Buzz Clifford recorded his only hit record *Baby Sittin' Boogie.* The initial release of the record gave the song's title of *Baby Sitter Boogie.*

Burt Bacharach

Gold record winning composer Burt Bacharach is the son of noted newspaper columnist Bert Bacharach. Burt's father was also a pro football player.

Bachman-Turner Overdrive

Bachman-Turner Overdrive took part of their name from the truckers' magazine *Overdrive.*

Back To School Again

In 1957 Timmie "Oh Yeah" Rogers recorded a stroll-dance titled *Back To School Again* which received a lot of air play on American Bandstand. Timmie Rogers then disappeared from the public for eighteen years only to reappear as a shoeshine boy on the television series "City of Angels."

La Verne Baker–Buddy Holly–Big Bopper

La Verne Baker, Buddy Holly, and the Big Bopper have all recorded similar follow-ups to their biggest hit releases. La Verne Baker recorded *Jim Dandy Got Married* as a follow up to her 1956 release *Jim Dandy;* Buddy Holly recorded *Peggy Sue Got Married* as follow-up to his 1958 hit *Peggy Sue;* and in 1959 the Big Bopper's follow-up to *Chantilly Lace* was *Big Bopper's Wedding.*

Lennie Baker

Sha Na Na's saxophonist Lennie Baker was once a member of the 1950s group Danny and the Juniors.

Florence Ballard

Florence Ballard, one of the original members of the Supremes, died in poverty in 1956. She passed away, a victim of a heart attack, at age thirty-two, on welfare at the time.

The Band

At 9:00 P.M. November 24, 1976 at San Francisco's Winterland, the Band announced that it was about to make its last public performance. From that performance came the 1978 outstanding movie, *The Last Waltz.* Their last song at the concert was *Don't Do It.*

Band on the Run

The people on the cover of the Paul McCartney and Wings album *Band on the Run* are: Paul McCartney, Linda McCartney, Denny Laine, Michael Parkinson

(British broadcaster), Kenny Lynch (musician), James Coburn (actor), Clement Freud (grandson of Sigmund Freud, and member of Parliament), Christoper Lee (actor), and John Contch (British light-heavyweight boxing champion).

Bands and Groups

Lead Artist	*"and the"*
Adam Faith	Roulettes
Adrian	Sunsets
Al Brown	Tunetoppers
Al Green	Soul Mates
Alexander	Greats
Alexander	Hamiltons
Alice Stewart	Soul Mates
Alicia	Rockaways
Allan	Flames
Alvin Cash	Registers/Crawlers
Amos Milburn	Chickenshackers
Andre Williams	Don Juans
Andy	Live Wires
Andy	Marglows
Angel	Devines
Angelo	Initials
Angie	Chicklettes
Anita	So & So's
Anna	"A" Train
Anne Murray	Richard
Anthony	Sophmores
Archie Bell	Drells
Arlene Smith	Chantels
Arthur Lee	Love
Arthur Lee Maye	Crowns

Lead Artist	*"and the"*
Attila	Huns
B. Brown	Rockin' McVouts
B. Bumble	Stingers
B. J. Thomas	Triumphs
Baby Huey	Babysitters
Baby Jane	Rockabyes
Baby Ray	Ferns
Barbara	Believers
Barbara	Browns
Barbarosa	Historians
Barry	Tamerlanes
Barry Manilow	City Rhythm (Vocal: Lady Flash)
Barry Petricoin	Belairs
Becky	Lollipops
Ben Gay	Silly Savages
Benny Barnes	Echoes
Benny Sharp	Sharpees
Bent Forcep	Patients
Bernadette	Swinging Bears
Bernie Kane	Rockin' Rhythms
Bert Conroy	Misfits
Bethea the Masked Man	Agents
Betty Jayne	Teenettes
Big Brother	Holding Company
Big Daddy	Little Sisters
Big Sis Andrews	Blues Busters
Big Wheelie	Hubcaps
Bill Deal	Rhondells
Bill Erwin	Four Jacks
Bill Haley	Comets
Bill Hershy	Almonds

Lead Artist	*"and the"*
Billie	Moonlighters
Billy	Echoes
Billy	Essentials
Billy	Fleet
Billy	Patio
Billy Abbott	Jewels
Billy Butler	Chanters
Billy Dee	Superchargers
Billy Dixon	Topics
Billy Fury	Blue Flames
Billy Huhn	Catalinas
Billy Joe	Checkmates
Billy Joe	Chessmen
Billy John	Continentals
Billy Jones	Teenettes
Billy J. Kramer	Coasters/Dakotas
Billy J. Spears	Stepchildren
Billy Joe Royal	Royal Blues
Billy Love	Lovers
Billy Mure	Karats/Trumpeteers
Billy Shears	All Americans
Billy Stewart	Soul Kings
Billy Ward	Dominoes
Bo Donaldson	Heywoods
Bob	Averones
Bob	Messengers
Bob Gerardi	Classic 4
Bob Kuban	In-Men
Bob Marley	Wailers
Bob Seger	Silver Bullet Band/ Last Heard
Bob B. Soxx	Blue Jeans
Bobbie	Beaus

Lead Artist	*"and the"*
Bobbie	Pleasers
Bobby	Consoles
Bobby	Orbits
Bobby	Velvets
Bobby Angel	Hillsiders
Bobby Day	Satellites
Bobby Gee	Celestials
Bobby Gregg	Friends
Bobby Lester	Moonlighters
Bobby Mathis	Sevilles
Bobby Maxwell	Exploits
Bobby Moore	Rhythm Aces
Bobby Picket	Crypt-Kickers Five
Bobby Taylor	Vancouvers
Bobby Vee	Shadows/Strangers
Bobby Womack	Peach
Bobsled	Tobaggans
Bonnie	Butterflys
Bonnie	Denims
Bonnie	Treasures
Bonnie Floyd	Original Untouchables
Brian Auger	Trinity/Oblivion Express
Brian Coll	Plattermen
Brian Poole	Tremeloes
Bruce Springsteen	"E" Street Band
Bud Dahsiell	Kingsmen
Bud Spudd	Sprouts
Buddy Holly	Crickets
Buddy Knox	Rhythm Orchids
Buddy Randell	Knickerbokers
Bull	Matadors
Bull Moose Jackson	Buffalo Bearcats
Butch Engle	Styx

Lead Artist	*"and the"*
Camile Howard	Boy Friends
Candy	Kisses
Cannibal	Headhunters
Captain Zap	Motortown Cut Ups
Captain Zoom	Androids
Carl	Commanders
Carl Mann	Kool Kats
Carry Grant	Grandeors
Cat Mother	All Night Newsboys
Cathy Jean	Roommates
Charley Hoss	Ponies
Cherry Vanilla	Staten Island Band
Chip	Quarter Tones
Chris Farlowe	Thunderbirds
Chuck Edwards	Five Crowns
Chuck Hicks	Count Downs
Chuck Rio	Originals
Cliff Richard	Shadows
Clinton Brook	B's
Collay	Satellites
Commander Cody	Lost Planet Airmen
Conlan	Crawlers
Conrad	Hurricane Strings
Conway Twitty	Lonely Blue Boys/ Twitty Birds
Cookie	Crumbs
Cookie	Cupcakes
Count	Colony
Count Lorry	Biters
Country Joe	Fish
Cubie	Five Stairsteps
Curtis Knight	Squires
D.D.T.	Repellents

Lead Artist	*"and the"*
Danny	Crowns
Danny	Dreamers
Danny	Hitmakers
Danny	Juniors
Danny	Memories
Danny	Saints
Danny	Velaires
Danny Peppermint	Jumping Jacks
Dante	Evergreens
Dante	Friends
Darrel	Oxfords
Darwin	Cupids
Dave Allen	Arrows
Dave Atkins	Offbeats
Dave Ebe	Rabin Band
Dave Edmunds	Rockpile
Dave Kennedy	Ambassadors
Dave Myers	Surftones
Dave T.	Del Rays
Davey Summers	Singing Ants
Danny Lamego	Jumpin' Jacks
Davey Hold	Hubcaps
David Bowie	Spiders from Mars/ Garson Band
David Camdanella	Dellchords
David Gates	Accents
Davie Jones	Daulphins
Deacon	Rock & Rollers
Debs	Escorts
Dee Jay	Runaways
Del	Escorts
Dennis Allen	Disco Turkeys
Dennis	Explorers

Lead Artist	*"and the"*
Dennis	Supertones
Dennis Yost	Classic IV
Denny	Dedications
Denny	LP's
Denny Laine	Diplomats
DeRoy Green	Cool Gents
Desmond Dekker	Aces
Dian	Greenbriar Boys
Dian James	Satisfactions
Diana Ross	Supremes
Diane	Darlettes
Dickey	Debonaires
Dickey Betts	Great Southern
Dickey Doo	Don'ts
Dickey Lee	Collegiates
Dino	Diplomats
Dion	Belmonts
Dion	Timberlanes
Dion	Wanderers
Dobie Gray	Chapter Four/Pollution
Dr. Feelgood	Interns
Dr. Hook	Medicine Show
Don	Galaxies
Don	Goodtimes
Don Carson	Whirlaways
Don Covay	Good Timers
Don Dell	Upstarts
Don Ellis	Royal Dukes
Don Hicks	Hot Licks
Don Ho	Aliis
Don Juan	Meadowlarks
Donald	Delighters
Donald Jenkins	Daylighters

Lead Artist	*"and the"*
Donnie	Cor-vets
Donnie	Darlingtons
Donnie	Del Chords
Donnie	Dreamers
Donny	Bi-Langos
Doug Donnell	Hot Rods
Dougie	Dolphins
Duane Eddy	Rebels
Duke Williams	Extremes
Dyke	Blazers
Ebe Sneezer	Epidemics
Eddie	Hot Rods
Eddie	Evergreens
Eddie	Starlites
Eddie Bell	Rock-a-fellas
Eddie Boyd	Chessmen
Eddie Cooley	Dimples
Edgar Winter	White Trash
Elmore James	Broomdusters
Elvis Costello	Attractions
Emmy Lou Harris	Hot Band
Eric Burdon	Animals/New Animals/ War
Eric Weissberg	Deliverance
Erik	Vikings
Ernie	Emperors
Ernie	Halos
Ernie K. Doe	Blue Diamonds
Etta James	Peaches
Ezra	Ivies
Fabian	Fabulous Four
Farrel	Flames
Fast Floyd	Firebirds

Lead Artist	*"and the"*
Ferlin Husky	Hush Puppies
Ferris	Wheels
Flash Cadillac	Continental Kids
Floyd & Jerry	Counterpoints
Frank Hubbell	Hubb-Caps
Frank Marino	Mahogany Rush
Frankie	Echoes
Frankie	Flips
Frankie	Timebreakers
Frankie Brent	Counts
Frankie Daye	Knights
Frankie Ervin	Spears
Frankie Lymon	Teenagers
Frankie Rossi	Dreams
Frankie Valli	Four Seasons
Fred Welsey	J. B.'s
Freddie	Dreamers
Freddy	Fat Boys
Freddy	Kinfolk
Gabriel	Angels
Gabriel	Teenage Choir
Gale Garnett	Gentle Reign
Garnet Mimms	Enchanters
Gary	Hornets
Gary	Nite Lites
Gary	Wombats
Gary Cane	Friends
Gary Haines	Five Sequins
Gary Lewis	Playboys
Gary Paxton	Road Runners
Gary Puckett	Union Gap
Gene Cornish	Unbeatables
Gene Fisher	Mystics

Lead Artist	*"and the"*
Gene Franklin	Spacemen
Gene Gray	Sting Rays
Gene Vincent	Blue Caps
George Fame	Blue Flames
George Perkins	Silver Stars
George Thorogood	Destroyers
George Torrence	Naturals
George Brown	Whipoorwills
Gerrand Kenny	New York Band
Gerry	Pacemakers
Ginger	Chiffons
Ginger Davis	Snaps
Gladys Knight	Pips
Gloria Walker	Chevelles
Goldie	Escorts
Goldie	Gingerbreads
Graham Parker	Rumours
Gram Parsons	Grevious Angels
Gregory Howard	Cadillacs
Guitar Slim	Playboys
Hank Ballard	Midnighters/Dapps
Harley	Night Riders
Harold Jenkins (Conway Twitty)	Rockhousers
Harold Melvin	Blue Notes
Harry	Croco-diles
Harry Hepcat	Boogie Woogie Band
Harvey	Moonglows
Harvey Scales	Seven Sounds
Herb Alpert	Tijuana Brass
Herb Lance	Classics
Herb Reed	Platters
Herbie	Class Cutters

Lead Artist	*"and the"*
Herman	Hermits
Honey Love	Love Notes
Hub Kapp	Wheels
Huey "Piano" Smith	Clowns
Hugh Barrett	Victors
Ian	Zodiacs
Ian Dury	Blockheads
Ian Hunter	Overnight Angels
Ichabod	Cranes
Iggy Pop	Stooges
Ike & Tina Turner	Family Vibes
Irene	Scotts
Isaac Hayes	Hot Buttered Soul
J.	Sabers
J. Frank Wilson	Cavaliers
Jack Ely	Courtmen
Jackie	Starlites
Jackie Brenston	Delta Cats
James Brown	Famous Flames
James T.	Workers
Jamie Coe	Gigolos
Jan	Radiants
Janis Joplin	Holding Company/ Full Tilt Boogie
Jay	Americans
Jay	Deltas
Jay	Techniques
Jay Bentley	Jet Set
Jaywalker	Pedestrians
Jean	Darlings
Jeanie	Boy Friends
Jeff	Ginos
Jeremy	Satyrs

Lead Artist	*"and the"*
Jerry	Attaches
Jerry	Landslides
Jerry	Radiants
Jerry	Upbeats
Jerry Butler	Impressions
Jerry Field	Lawyers
Jewel	Rubies
Jimmy	Illusions
Jimmy	Rebels
Jimmy	Roadrunners
Jimmy Buffett	Coral Reefer Band
Jimmy Cavello	House Rockers
Jimmy Clanton	Rockets
Jimmy Coe	Gay Cats of Rhythm
Jimmy Gartin	Swingers
Jimmy Gilmer	Fireballs
Jimmy Hayes	Soul Surfers
Jimmy J.	J's
Jimmy James	Candy Canes
Jimmy James	Vagabonds
Jimmy Jay	Blue Falcons
Jimmy Jones	Pretenders
Jimmy Lee	Earls
Jimmy Liggins	Drops of Joy
Jimmy Norman	Hollywood Teenagers
Jimmy Witherspoon	Quintones
Joe Bennet	Sparklestones
Joe Boot	Winds
Joe Capp	Starfires
Joe Cocker	Cock 'n' Bull
Joe Darenbourg	Dixie Flyers
Joe Dee	Tophands
Joe Dodo	Groovers

Lead Artist	*"and the"*
Joe Liggins	Honeydrippers
Joe Walsh	Barnstorm
Joey	Continentals
Joey	Lexingtons
Joey	Teenagers
Joey	Twisters
Joey Dee	Starlighters
John Buck	Blazers
John Denver	Fat City
John Entwhistle	Ox
John Fred	Starlighters
John Fred	Playboy Band
John Hammond	Playboy Band
John Hill	Piemen
John Lee Hooker	Coast To Coast Blues Band
John Mayall	Bluesbreakers
Johnny	Dreams
Johnny	Hurricanes
Johnny	Jammers
Johnny	Jokers
Johnny	Screaming Nighthawks
Johnny	Tokens
Johnny	Vibratones
Johnny Ace	Beale Streeters
Johnny Brisco	Little Beavers
Johnny Christmas	Dynamics
Johnny Coe	Reptiles
Johnny Edwards	White Caps
Johnny Garrett	Rising Signs
Johnny George	Girlfriends
Johnny Greco	Davies
Johnny Johnson	Bandwagon
Johnny Jones	Catalinas

Lead Artist	*"and the"*
Johnny Kidd	Pirates
Johnny Knight	Kingsmen
Johnny Moore	Three Blazers
Jules	Polar Bears
Jumping Judge	Court
Junior	Attractions
Junior	Friends
Jr. Walker	All-Stars
K. C.	Sunshine Band
K. C. Grand	Shades
Kathy Young	Innocents
Kayo	Trinities
Kenny	Fiends
Kenny	Kasuals
Kenny	Modads
Kenny	Socialites
Kenny	Whalers
Kenny Esquire	Starlites
Kenny Rogers	First Edition
Kevin Ayers	Soporifies
King Curtis	Kingpins/Noble Knights
King George	Checkmates
Kipper	Exciters
Kit	Outlaws
Kool	Gang
Kris Kristofferson	Band of Thieves
Lafayette	Lasabres
La Verne Baker	Gliders
Lance Loud	Mumps
Lancelo	Legends
Larry	Legends
Larry	Standards
Lee Andrews	Hearts

Lead Artist	*"and the"*
Lenny	Chimes
Lenny	Continentals
Leo	Duets
Leo De Lyon	Musclemen
Leon	Metronomes
Leon Russell	Gap Band
Leroy	Rocky Fellers
Levi	Rockats
Lewis Lymon	Teen Chords
Levy Melton	Dey Brothers
Lil June	Januarys
Lincoln Fig	Dates
Linda Ronstadt	Stone Poneys
Link Wray	Wraymen
Lisa	Lullabies
Little Anthony	Imperials
Little Bernie	Cavaliers
Little Bill	Bluenotes
Little Bob	Lollipops
Little Caesar	Romans
Little Clyde	Teens
Little E	Mello Tone 3
Little Esther	Robins
Little Guy	Giants
Little Jan	Radiants
Little Jimmy	Tops
Little Joe	Thrillers
Little Joe	Morrocos
Little Joey	Flips
Little John	Sherwoods
Little Julian	Tigers
Little Louie	Lovers
Little Man	Victors

Lead Artist	*"and the"*
Little Marcus	Devotions
Little Nate	Chryslers
Little Pete	Youngsters
Little Richard	Upsetters
Little Roger	Goosebumps
Little Romeo	Casanovas
Little Ronnie	Chromatics
Little Sunny Day	Clouds
Little Ted	Novas
Little Tom	Valentines
Little Tommy	Elgins
Little Victor	Vistas
Little Walter	Jukes/Night Cats
Little Willie	Adolescents
Lonnie	Carrollons
Lonnie	Crisis
Lonnie	Legends
Lothar	Hand People
Lou Berry	Bel Raves
Louis Brooks	Hi-Toppers
Louis Jordon	Tympany Five
Lugee	Lions
Lulu	Luvers
Luther Bond	Emeralds
Mad Mike	Maniacs
Malcolm Dodds	Tune Drops
Manuel	Renegades
Marc Bolan	T. Rex
Marc Cavell	Classmates
Marie	Deccors
Mario	Flips
Mark	Escorts
Martha (Reeves)	Vandellas

Lead Artist	*"and the"*
Marty	Symbols
Marty Jay	Surfin' Cats
Maurice Williams	Zodiacs
Max Frost	Troopers
Memphis Slim	House Rockers
Michael	Continentals
Michael Franks	Crusaders
Michael Zager	Moon Band
Mickey Farrel	Dynamics
Mike	Ravens
Mike	Utopians
Mike Berry	Outlaws
Mike Gordon	Agates
Mike McGear	Scaffold
Mike Lymon	Little People
Mike Patterson	Fugitives
Mr. Acker Bilk	Paramount Jazz Band
Mister Bassman	Symbols
Mitch Ryder	Detroit Wheels
Moose	Pelicans
Morry Williams	Kids
Morty Jay	Surferin' Cats
Nat "King" Cole	Four Knights
Nat Kendrick	Swans
Neal	Newcomers
Neil Young	Crazy Horse/Stray Gators
Nick Harris	Soundbarriers
Nick Lowe	Rockpile
Nick Marco	Venetians
Nicky	Nacks
Nicky	Nobles
Nicky Addeo	Darchaes/Uniques
Nicky De Matteo	Sorrows

Lead Artist	*"and the"*
Nino	Ebb Tides
Nolan Strong	Diablos
Norman Fox	Rob-Roys
Ola	Janglers
Oliver	Twisters
Ollie	Nightingales
Omar	Village Idiots
Pat	Satellites
Pat	Wildcats
Pat Cordell	Crescents
Patsy	Beatniks
Patty	Emblems
Patty LaBelle	Blue Belles
Patty Lace	Petticoats
Patty McCoy	Renegades
Paul Butterfield	Better Days
Paul McCartney	Wings
Paul Revere	Raiders
Pearl Harbor	Explosions
Penny Baker	Pillows
Peter Debree	Wanderers
Peter Jarett	Fifth Circle
Phil	Frantics
Phil Gary	Rock & Roll Zoo
Prince Albert	Cans
Question Mark	Mysterians
Ral Donner	Starfires
Randy	Rainbows
Randy	Rockets
Ray	Darchaes
Ray Allen	Upbeats
Ray Campi	Rockabilly Rebels
Renee Rambles	Rhinestones

Lead Artist	*"and the"*
Reparata	Delrons
Ria	Reasons
Ria	Revellons
Rich	Bags
Rich	Keens
Rich	Rays
Richard	Young Lions
Richard Berry	Dreamers
Richard Hell	Voidoids
Richie	Saxons
Richie	Royals
Rick	Keens
Rick	Legends
Rick	Masters
Rick	Raiders
Rick	Randells
Rick	Rick-A-Shays
Rick Dees	Cast of Idiots
Rick James	Stone City Band
Rick Nelson	Stone Canyon Band
Rickie	Hallmarks
Ricky	Saints
Ricky Dee	Embers
Rico	Ravens
Rita Coolidge	Dixie Flyers
Robby	Robbins
Robert Gordon	Wildcats
Robin	Three Hoods
Robin Hood	Merrymen
Rochell	Candels
Rod Bernard	Twisters
Rodney	Blazers
Rodney Baker	Chantiers

Lead Artist	*"and the"*
Ronald Desoto	Studebakers
Ronnie	Crayons
Ronnie	Delaires
Ronnie	Dirt Riders
Ronnie	Hi-Lites
Ronnie	Manhattans
Ronnie	Pomona Casuals
Ronnie	Premiers
Ronnie	Relatives
Ronnie	Schoolmates
Ronnie Cates	Travellers
Ronnie Hawkins	Hawks
Ronnie Jones	Classmates
Ronnie Premiere	Royal Lancers
Ronnie Vare	Inspirations
Ronny	Daytonas
Rory Storm	Texans/Hurricanes
Rosie	Originals
Roxy	Daychords
Roy Buchannon	Snake Stretchers
Roy Head	Traits
Roy Loney	Phantom Movers
Roy Milton	Solid Senders
Roy Orbison	Teen Kings/Roses/ Candymen
Ruby	Romantics
Ruby Star	Grey Ghost
Ruth Brown	Rhythm-Makers
Sal	Watchers
Sally	Roses
Sally	Sallycats
Sam the Sham	Pharoahs
Sam Space	Cadets

Lead Artist	*"and the"*
Sami Jo	Candy Mountain
Sammy	Del-Lands
Sammy Hagan	Viscounts
Sammy Wilde	Dust Cloud
Sandy	Cupids
Scott English	Accents
Sergio Mendes	Brasil '66/Brasil '77/ Brasil '88
Shadden	King Lears
Shep	Limelites
Shirley Gunter	Queens
Shu Shu	Space Jockeys
Simon Stokes	Nighthawks
Siouxsie	Banshees
Ski-King	Life Buoys
Skippy	Hi-Lites
Sly	Family Stone
Smokey Robinson	Miracles
Sonny Charles	Checkmates, Ltd.
Sonny Gee	Standells
Sonny Patterson	Pastel Six
Sonny Till	Orioles
Southside Johnny	Asbury Jukes
Spanky	Our Gang
Spongy	Dolls
Stephen Stills	Manassas
Steve	Emperors
Steve Alairo	Redcoats
Steve Gibson	Red Cape
Stevie Wonder	Wonderlove
Sticks McGhee	Buddies
Sunnie	Minor Chords
Sunny	Sunglows

Lead Artist	*"and the"*
Sunny	Sunliners
Susie	4 Trumpets
Suzy	Red Stripes
Sylvester	Hot Band
Tandi	Teamates
Ted Nugent	Amboy Dukes
Teddy	Continentals
Teddy	Pandas
Teddy	Patches
Teddy	Twilights
Terry	Mellows
Terry	Tags
Terry	Tunisians
Terry	Tyrants
Terry Gilkyson	Easy Riders
Terry Knight	Pack
Tex	Chex
Thurston Harris	Sharps
Tico	Triumphs
Tim Tam	Turn-Ons
Timmy Lymon	Tellers
Tino	Revlons
Tiny Tim	Hits
Todd Rundgren	Utopia
Tom Austin	Healeys
Tom Glazer	Children's Chorus
Tom Petty	Heartbreakers
Tom Scott	L. A. Express
Tom Thumb	Casuals
Tommy Burk	Counts
Tommy Faia	True Blue Facts
Tommy Genoa	Precisions
Tommy James	Shondells

Lead Artist	*"and the"*
Tommy Vann	Echoes
Tommy Roe	Romans
Tony	Day Dreams
Tony	Holidays
Tony	Raindrops
Tony	Technics
Tony	Twilights
Tony Carmen	Spitfires
Tony Cotton	Concords
Tony Dee	Pageants
Tony Harris	Woodies
Tony Maresco	Dynamics
Toots	Maytals
Trudy Williams	Six Teens
Ty Stewart	Jokers
Tyrone	Nu-Ports
Valentine	Lovers
Vince Martin	Tarriers
Vito	Hands
Vito	Salutations
Wally Lee	Storms
Walter Murphy	Big Apple Band
Wayne	Exceptions
Wayne Cochran	C .C. Riders
Wayne County	Back Street Boys/ Electric Chairs
Wayne Fontana	Mindbenders
Willie	Wheels
Willie Alexander	Boom Boom Band
Willie Winfield	Harptones
Wini Brown	Boy Friends
Yolanda	Naturals
Zip	Zippers

Bang Records

The New York City based Bang Records (one of their biggest releases was *Hang On Sloopy* by the McCoys in 1965) was founded by four record producers. The name Bang was derived from the first letters of the first name of each partner. The founders were: *B*ert Berns, *A*hmet Ertegun, *N*esuhi Ertegun, *G*erald "Jerry" Wexler.

Barbara Ann

The original version of *Barbara Ann,* recorded by the Regents in 1961, was actually released after the group no longer existed. The record sat around the studio months after the group recorded it. After the group broke up, the demo was discovered and then became a hit for a group that didn't exist.

In 1965 a live cut from the *Beach Boys' Party* album became a hit record, reviving the Regents originally recorded version of *Barbara Ann.* The song was a hit for the Beach Boys, but it was Dean Torrence (of Jan and Dean) who sang lead on the song.

Len Barry

Len Barry, who in 1965 had a hit with *1-2-3* was previously the lead singer of the Philadelphia group the Dovells, who had a hit in 1961 titled *Bristol Stomp.*

The Battle of New Orleans

Johnny Horton's number-one hit record in 1960, *The Battle of New Orleans,* was banned on Canadian radio while Queen Elizabeth visited the country that year.

It was composed by Jimmy Driftwood and based on the folk tune *The Eighth of January.*

Jeff Baxter

Guitarist Jeff "Skunk" Baxter played for both Steely Dan and the Doobie Brothers.

Bay City Rollers

The Scottish group Bay City Rollers named themselves by putting a pin in a world map. The pin ended up on Bay City, Michigan.

Prior to their hit *Bye Bye Baby* (originally recorded by the Four Seasons), the Bay City Rollers didn't play the instruments on their records. The music was performed by studio musicians. The group did provide their own music on *Bye Bye Baby* and thereafter.

Beach Boys

It was the Beach Boys who sang the theme song for the 1964 television series "Karen" starring Debbie Watson.

Carl Wilson, Al Jardine, and Dennis Wilson sang back up on Chicago's *Wishing You Were Here.*

Carl Wilson and Bruce Johnson sang on America's *Hat Trick* album.

Beachwood 4-5789

In 1962 the Marvelettes recorded the catchy song *Beachwood 4-5789*. In 1966 Wilson Pickett recorded his version—updated with a new digited prefix—titled *634-5789*.

Beale Streeters

During the early 1950s an obscure R&B group was formed without much success. Some of the members of that group were: B. B. King, Bobby Bland, Johnny Ace, and Earl Forrest.

Beatle Nut

To celebrate the Beatles' first American tour in 1964, Baskin-Robbins created a new flavor of ice cream—Beatle Nut.

The Beatles

Stu Sutcliffe was the group's member who gave them the name Beetles with John Lennon changing the spelling.

When Vee Jay Records first began to release the Beatles' early hit songs in the U.S., they grouped them on an album with the Four Seasons, titling the LP *The International Battle of the Century*.

It took the Beatles twelve hours to record their first album *Please Please Me* in 1963. Four years later in 1967 it took the group over 700 hours to record *Sergeant Pepper's Lonely Hearts Club Band*.

When Vee Jay records released *Please Please Me*, their first Beatles single in the U.S. in 1963, the group's name was misspelled on the record label as The Beattles.

The last album that the Beatles recorded together was not the last album released. *Abbey Road* was the final recording of the Beatles, yet *Let It Be* was released after it.

The Beatles have had their records released on the following record labels in the U. S.: Capitol, Swan, Decca, Vee Jay, Tollie, MGM, Polydor, Atco, and Apple.

Most Beatles fans can recall the group's drummer prior to Ringo Starr. It was Pete Best who was fired to make room for Starr, who had been the drummer for Rory Storm and the Hurricanes. But prior to Best, who drummed for the Beatles? First there was Tommy Moore who was forced to quit the group by his girl friend. Then there was six-foot-two-inch Norman Chapman, an excellent musician, who had to leave the Beatles upon being drafted into the British Army. That brings us up to Pete Best.

Bee Gees

The Bee Gees set a record in 1978 by having seven number-one hit singles in a six-month period. The record they broke was previously held by the Beatles.

Prior to becoming the Bee Gees, the fraternal group called themselves the Blue Cats.

Maurice and Robin Gibb are twin brothers.

The Bee Gees composed *More Than A Woman* for the Tavares, *If I Can't Have You* for Yvonne Elliman, *Warm Ride* for Rare Earth, and *Emotion* for Samantha Sang.

During the week of February 25 to March 4, 1978, the Bee Gees and their compositions held the top five chart positions in the U. S.:

1. *Stayin' Alive*	Bee Gees
2. *How Deep Is Your Love*	Bee Gees
3. *Night Fever*	Bee Gees
4. *Love Is Thicker Than Water*	Andy Gibb (composers)
5. *Emotion*	Samantha Sang (composers)

Actually, the origin of the group's name isn't simply the initials of the Brothers Gibb. Two people who helped the young brothers were disc jockey Bill Gates and a friend Bill Goode, who (along with Barry Gibb) all shared the same initials—B. G. It was Bill Gates who named the group the Bee Gees.

Harry Belafonte

Harry Belafonte was the first singer to win an Emmy.

It was Belafonte, who in 1956 had a number of very successful calypso songs including *Day-O* and *Jamaica-Farewell,* whose singing voice was dubbed in by LeVern Hutcherson in the 1954 movie *Carmen Jones.*

Belafonte's *Calpyso* LP is the first album ever to sell a million copies.

Bob Dylan played harmonica on Harry Belafonte's version of *Midnight Special.*

Archie Bell

When *Tighten Up* entered the charts in 1968, Archie Bell was in Vietnam fighting for the U.S. Army. It was not until he was convalescing in a Korean hospital from a leg wound that he learned that *Tighten Up* was the number-one record back home.

Archie Bell, lead singer of Archie Bell and the Drells, is the brother of Rick Bell, a former all-American at U.C.L.A., who played halfback for the Tampa Bay Buccaneers.

Jesse Belvin

In 1955 Jesse Belvin provided all the voices on the Federal release *So Fine,* credited on the label to the Sheiks.

In 1956 a single titled *Girl of My Dreams* was released by a four-man vocal group the Cliques. It was discovered that the four voices on the record were actually those of Jesse Belvin. The record was later released under Jesse Belvin's name.

In 1957 Jesse Belvin not only recorded a cover version of Sam Cooke's current hit *You Send Me* but he also covered the flip side *Summertime* as well.

Jesse Belvin was also a member of the Shields who's only hit, *You Cheated,* was recorded in 1958.

Tony Bennett

Due to the popularity of Tony Bennett's ballad *I Left My Heart in San Francisco,* the singer now has both a plaza and a terrace named for him in lovely San Francisco. Although *I Left My Heart in San Francisco* became a hit in 1962, the song was composed years earlier by George Cory and Douglas Cross. It took the composers eight years getting someone to record it.

Brook Benton

Aside from being a successful soloist and singing several duets with Dinah Washington, Brook Benton composed the 1958 Nat "King" Cole hit *Looking Back* and the 1962 Clyde McPhatter hit *Lover Please.*

Chuck Berry

Chuck Berry is a graduate of the Gibbs Beauty School, with a degree in cosmetology.

Near St. Louis, Missouri, Chuck Berry has built an amusement park aptly named Berry Park.

Rocker Chuck Berry spent two years (1962-1964) in a state penitentiary after being convicted for violation of the Mann Act.

Martha, his sister, can be heard singing on her brother's recordings of *Come On* and *Go Go Go.*

In 1979 Chuck Berry was sentenced to a 120-day term in a federal prison for income tax evasion.

Jan Berry

Half of the duet of Jan and Dean, Jan Berry can boast an I.Q. of 185, which puts him in the genius range.

Richard Berry

Singer Richard Berry has not been well known to most rock 'n' roll followers, yet he has been heard on a number of hit records. It was Berry who sang lead on the Robins' (later named the Coasters) 1954 hits *Riot in Cell Block #9* and *Smokey Joe's Cafe*. Berry could also be heard on Etta James' recording of *Dance With Me Henry*. In 1957 Richard Berry had his first solo hit record, the original version of the classic *Louie, Louie*.

Pete Best

Ringo Starr replaced the Beatles' drummer Pete Best prior to the group's recording their first hit record. Pete, in later years, needing money and fame, recorded an album cleverly titled *Best of the Beatles*.

Best of My Love

Two different songs with the same title have reached the number-one position on the charts: the Eagles' *Best of My Love* (#1 in 1975): the Emotions' *Best of My Love* (#1 in 1977).

Big Bad John

When Jimmy Dean's hit record *Big Bad John* was first released in 1962, the lyrics included the words "one hell of a man." But because of the word "hell," the song was temporarily withdrawn from public release, returning with the "cleaner" lyrics "a big, big man." It still reached the number-one position.

Big Bad John was one of President John F. Kennedy's favorite songs.

The metal clanging sound heard in *Big Bad John* was provided by Floyd Cramer.

Big Bopper

J. P. Richardson, who recorded under the name Big Bopper, only had one hit record (*Chantilly Lace*) but is immortalized because of the tragedy that took his life along with that of Buddy Holly and Ritchie Valens. Prior to becoming the Big Bopper, Richardson had composed two hit records: *Running Bear* (a Johnny Preston hit) and *White Lightning* (a George Jones hit). In 1957 under the name of Jape Richardson (and the Japetts) he recorded the two songs *Begger To A King* and *Teenage Moon.*

The Big Bopper once held the world record for continuous broadcasting by a disc jockey—122 hours, 8 minutes. The event took place at radio station KTRM in Beaumont, Texas, in 1956.

The flip side, *The Purple People Eater Meets the Witch Doctor,* was written by Joe South.

Jiles Perry Richardson was his actual name.

Billboard Top 100

On April 4, 1964 the Billboard Top 100 chart started off like this:

#1	Can't Buy Me Love	Beatles	Capitol
#2	Twist and Shout	Beatles	Tollie
#3	She Loves You	Beatles	Swan
#4	I Want To Hold Your Hand	Beatles	Capitol

#5	Please Please Me	Beatles	Vee Jay

The Beatles also occupied slots #16, #44, #49, #69, #74, #84, and #89.

Bird Groups

Here are some noted groups which were named after bird collectives: Eagles, Falcons, Robins, Larks, Crows, Swallows, Meadowlarks, Penguins, Hawks, Ravens, Flamingos, Orioles, and Cardinals.

Stephen Bishop

The title track from the popular 1978 movie *Animal House* was penned by Stephen Bishop. He played a bit role as a folk singer in the film.

Black

Drummer Ed Cassidy of Spirit, like Johnny Cash, always wears black when he performs.

Bill Black

The man who played bass guitar on Elvis Presley's 1956 hit record *Don't Be Cruel* would four years later have a hit instrumental version of the same song. The man was Bill Black.

His brother Johnny Black played bass for the Johnny Burnette Trio. Johnny joined the trio after Dorsey Burnette left to begin a solo career.

Cilla Black

Cilla Black's real name is Priscilla White.

Cilla Black was discovered by Brian Epstein when she both sang and worked as a hatcheck girl in Liverpool's famed Cavern Club. She worked there at the time the Beatles were just beginning.

Black Sabbath—The Mindbenders

The rock band Black Sabbath named themselves after the 1964 Boris Karloff movie *Black Sabbath.* Previously Wayne Fontana's backup group, the Mindbenders named themselves after the 1962 British horror movie *The Mind Benders.*

Blood, Sweat and Tears

The 1970 Barbra Streisand–George Segal movie *The Owl and the Pussycat* was scored by Blood, Sweat and Tears.

Blue Monday

The inspiration for Fats Domino's 1956 hit *Blue Monday* came from the name of a New Orleans club, where he played with Dave Bartholomew's band in 1949, called the Blue Monday Club.

Blue Ridge Rangers

Upon the demise of the Creedence Clearwater Revival, John Fogerty started recording with a country band called the Blue Ridge Rangers. In reality, the group was Fogerty playing all the instruments and singing all the vocals.

Blue Suede Shoes

Carl Perkins' version of 1956 hit *Blue Suede Shoes* is the first record to ever have made the pop charts, the country charts, and the R&B charts at the same time.

Blue Suede Shoes—Honey Don't

It has got to be a compliment to a composer/artist to have the greatest rock 'n' roll artist and greatest rock group cut a cover of his work. In 1956 Carl Perkins recorded the two-sided Sun label hit *Blue Suede Shoes* and *Honey Don't.* Elvis successfully covered *Blue Suede Shoes,* while the Beatles recorded *Honey Don't.*

Blues Brothers

The Blues Brothers were originally created as a parody of a rock group for the television series "Saturday Night, Live."

Bobby Bland

Bobby Bland was once a chauffeur for both singers B. B. King and Junior Parker.

Bobby Bland and Johnny Ace played for the same band, led by Adolph Duncan, in the early 1950s.

Tommy Bolin

Tommy Bolin, who died on December 4, 1977, was buried wearing a ring that Jimi Hendrix had worn on the day he died.

Gary "U.S." Bonds

On the first hit singles by "U.S." Bonds (real name, Gary Anderson), *New Orleans* and *Quarter to Three,* the artist's name was credited "by," so that his name would read as the pun, "By U.S. Bonds."

Daniel Boone

Both Pat Boone and Lovin' Spoonful member Steve Boone claim to be descended from the frontiersman Daniel Boone.

Pat Boone

Pat Boone served as student body president of David Lipscomb High School and was twice voted the Most Popular Boy. Shirley Foley, Pat's future wife, was the Homecoming Queen.

Country great Red Foley is the father-in-law of singer Pat Boone.

Crooner Pat Boone was one of the owners of Oakland Oaks Basketball team of the ABA. The team no longer exists.

Born To Be Wild

Steppenwolf's *Born To Be Wild* can be heard on the sound track of both the motion pictures *Easy Rider* (1969) and *Coming Home* (1978).

Boston

In 1976 the unknown group Boston sold over a million copies of their debut album in only two-and-a-half months.

Tom Scholz, lead of the group Boston, has a Master's Degree from M.I.T.

Both Sides Now

Judy Collins' hit *Both Sides Now* (1968) was composed by Joni Mitchell.

Angie Bowie

It was for David Bowie's wife, Angie, that Mick Jagger composed the song *Angie.*

David Bowie

Singer David Bowie named his son Zowie. Zowie Bowie!

When performing, David Bowie at times wears a baseball cap which was given to him by baseball great Mickey Rivers.

Singer David Bowie's real name is David Jones, but he was forced to change it because there was already another musician on the scene named Davy Jones, a member of the Monkees. This is much like the problem actor Stewart Granger encountered, having to change from his real name James Stewart.

Judy Bowles

Judy Bowles was the girl friend for whom Brian Wilson wrote the Beach Boys' 1963 hit *Surfer Girl.*

Patty Boyd

Patty Boyd has been married to two superstars: George Harrison and Eric Clapton, both highly respected lead guitarists.

Bonnie Bramlett

Soulful singer Bonnie Bramlett was once a member of Ike and Tina Turner's backup vocal group the Ikettes.

Breaking Up Is Hard To Do

There is only one case of an artist recording a rock song and then years later recording the same song as a ballad. That is exactly what Neil Sedaka did when he first recorded *Breaking Up Is Hard To Do* in 1962 as a rocker and then revised the song as a ballad in 1975. Both times the song became a good seller.

Walter Brennan

Even three-time Academy Award winner (three Best Supporting Actor Oscars) Walter Brennan had a hit record in 1960 with *Dutchman's Gold.* To prove that he wasn't just a one-hit artist, he made the charts again in 1962 with *Old Rivers.*

Teresa Brewer

At age five saucy Teresa Brewer made an appearance on "Major Bowes Original Amateur Hour" on radio.

Those Red Heads from Seattle (1953) is Teresa Brewer's only movie appearance.

Bridge Over Troubled Waters

Larry Knechtel of the group Bread is the piano player on Simon and Garfunkel's 1970 record *Bridge Over Troubled Waters.*

Geoff Britton

Wings' member Geoff Britton represented Britain in the first International Karate Championships, held in Japan.

Bromley Technical

Bromley Technical High School in Beckenham, Kent, England, is the school that future rock stars Peter Frampton and David Bowie attended as fellow students. Pete's father Owen Frampton, an art teacher there, had Bowie as one of his students. Frampton and Bowie played in rival bands, David Bowie with George and the Dragons, and Peter Frampton with the Little Ravens.

Brother Records

The only artists (other than the label's owners the Beach Boys) to record for Brother Records was the South African group Flame.

Arthur Brown

Bizarre performer Arthur Brown, billed as The Crazy World of Arthur Brown, has a Ph.D. in philosophy from Cambridge.

James Brown

James Brown in his youth spent three years in a Georgia reform school.

Although he's been recording for over twenty years and has numerous top-ten records, James Brown has never had a number-one record.

"Soul Brother Number One," James Brown, nicknamed his private Lear jet, the Sex Machine.

James Brown in his youth won sixteen out of seventeen professional bantamweight boxing matches.

As a young lad, James Brown shined shoes in various locations in Augusta, Georgia. One of his favorite spots was outside radio station WRDW. Today James Brown is the owner of that radio station.

Jackson Browne

Jackson Browne was one of the original members of the Nitty Gritty Dirt Band.

Anita Bryant

When Anita Bryant was born, she was pronounced dead by her family doctor. Only after being dunked in icy water was she revived.

When Anita Bryant became a runner-up for the Miss America Contest, one of the judges was Mitch Miller, who previously had turned down Anita Bryant for a recording contract when she was fourteen.

Lindsey Buckingham

Lindsey Buckingham, a member of the highly popular group Fleetwood Mac, has a brother named Greg who won an Olympic medal in the 1968 Olympics.

The Buddy Holly Story

Gary Busey performed magnificently when he portrayed the late Buddy Holly in the 1978 movie *The*

Buddy Holly Story. Not only did Busey look like Holly, but he did a perfect vocal imitation.

In the movie *The Buddy Holly Story* a strange phenomenon occurred. All the artists portrayed in the film met tragic deaths; Buddy Holly—died in a plane crash; The Big Bopper—died in a plane crash; Ritchie Valens—died in a plane crash; Sam Cooke—shot to death; King Curtis—stabbed to death; Eddie Cochran—died in a London taxicab.

Buffalo Springfield

Contrary to popular belief, Buffalo Springfield was *not* named for two cities. The legendary group was more romantically named for a steamroller.

Solomon Burke

Soul artist Solomon Burke was a child evangelist, preaching on local radio and in Solomon's temple at age nine. He was billed as the Wonder Boy Preacher.

Burnette Brothers

Johnny and Dorsey Burnette once worked for the same Memphis company for which Elvis Presley drove a truck, the Crown Electric Company. Both brothers have composed songs for teenage idol Ricky Nelson.

Johnny Burnette

Johnny Burnette was once a Golden Gloves Boxing Champion.

Before Bill Black and Scotty Moore became the back-up for Elvis Presley, they performed with Johnny Burnette.

Gary Busey

Gary Busey, who portrayed the late Buddy Holly in the 1978 movie *The Buddy Holly Story,* was once a drummer in Leon Russell's band (under the name of Teddy Jack Eddy).

Butterscotch Castle Records

The Captain and Tenille's first record *The Way I Want To Touch You* was originally recorded on a record label formed by the husband and wife team, which they named Butterscotch Castle Records (named for their apartment house). The pair later recorded a song also titled *Butterscotch Castle.*

The Byrds

The Byrds have been credited with recording both the first folk-rock song, *Mr. Tambourine Man,* and the first country-rock album, *Sweetheart of the Rodeo,* in 1968.

Prior to adopting the name the Byrds, the Los Angeles based song group was known as the Beefeaters.

At the same time as the Byrds popularity, a British group emerged calling themselves the Birds. The Birds didn't fly, but the Byrds did, straight to the top of the charts.

Buzz Buzz Buzz

In 1957 the Hollywood Flames had one hit record with *Buzz Buzz Buzz*. The lead singer on the record was Bobby Day, who as a solo artist had success with hits such as *Rockin' Robin, Over and Over,* and *Little Bitty Pretty One.*

C

Cadence Records

During the 1950s a New York City based record company named Cadence Records handled the music of Andy Williams, the Chordettes, Julius La Rosa, the Everly Brothers, Link Wray and others. The label was founded by bandleader Archie Bleyer after he had been fired on the air on October 19, 1953, along with Julius La Rosa, by television host Arthur Godfrey.

The Cadets

Stranded in the Jungle was a rocking song recorded by the Cadets in 1956. When the group recorded ballad material, such as *Why Don't You Write Me,* they did so under the name the Jacks. The Jacks were the backup vocal group on Paul Anka's first record, *I Confess,* on RPM Records, released in 1956.

Barbara Campbell

Barbara Campbell was the pseudonym under which Lou Adler, Herb Alpert and Sam Cooke composed

Wonderful World and *Everybody Loves to Cha Cha Cha,* two hits for Cooke.

In actuality, Barbara Campbell was the name of the girl Sam Cooke met in high school, later making her his wife.

Glen Campbell

Prior to becoming a highly popular solo artist, Glen Campbell played guitar in sessions for Nat "King" Cole, Dean Martin, Frank Sinatra, and Sammy Davis, Jr., among others.

Glen Campbell has played for both the Champs and the Beach Boys. On the Beach Boys' *Good Vibrations* Glen played lead guitar.

Canadian Groups

In the 1950s, years prior to the British rock invasion of the 1960s, two Canadian groups covered numerous rhythm and blues hits such as those by the Penguins, the Del Vikings, the Gladiolas, and the Rays. Those two Canadian groups were the Diamonds and the Crew Cuts, both of which recorded for Mercury Records.

The vocal group the Four Lads, who, besides backing Johnnie Ray on his hits, had several chart songs of their own in the 1950s, also hailed from Canada.

Candles in the Rain

On Melanie's 1970 hit *Lay Down* (*Candles in the Rain*), the voices you hear in the background belong to the Edwin Hawkins singers.

The Candy Man

Sammy Davis, Jr.'s first number-one song, *The Candy Man* (1972), was taken from the 1971 movie *Willy Wonka and the Chocolate Factory.* The song was written by singer Anthony Newley.

Freddy Cannon

Born Fredrick Anthony Picariello, Freddy "Boom Boom" Cannon played guitar on the G-Clefs' 1956 hit *Ka-Ding-Dong.*

Canonsburg, Pennsylvania

Both crooners Perry Como (born in 1912) and Bobby Vinton (born in 1941) hail from the Pennsylvania town of Canonsburg.

Can't Help Falling in Love

Elvis Presley closed all his concerts with the lovely ballad *Can't Help Falling in Love* from his 1961 movie *Blue Hawaii.*

Captain and Tennille

The Captain (Daryl Dragon) and his wife and partner Toni Tennille are both vegetarians.

The backup vocal group of the Captain and Tennille is composed of Toni Tennille's three sisters, Melissa, Louisa, and Jane.

The Captain's father, Carmen Dragon, was the conductor for the Hollywood Bowl Symphony while Frank Tennille, the father of Toni, played as a member of Bob Crosby's Bob Cats.

It was Beach Boy Mike Love that gave Daryl the nickname of "The Captain," when Daryl played organ for the group.

Toni Tennille is the only Beach Girl in the history of the Beach Boys group.

Vicki Carr

Vicki Carr provided the singing voice for Cyd Charisse in the 1966 Matt Helm (Dean Martin) movie, *The Silencers.*

Kris Carson

Prior to his American debut as a singer, Kris Kristofferson recorded in Britain under the name Kris Carson.

Clarence Carter

Clarence Carter, who had the hits *Slip Away* (1968) and *Patches* (1970), became blind at age one.

Al Casey

Just as Bobby Bare was credited on his 1959 hit *All American Boy* as Bill Parsons, so guitarist Al Casey's 1961 release *Caravan Part 1 & 2* was mistakenly credited to Duane Eddy on the Gregmark 5 label.

Johnny Cash

Country singer Johnny Cash sang the theme song *Johnny Yuma* for the television series "The Rebel" starring Nick Adams.

Johnny Cash's late mother-in-law was Maybelle Carter, June Carter's mother.

Shaun Cassidy

Rock singer Shaun Cassidy, who played Joe Hardy on the television series "The Hardy Boys," is the younger stepbrother of singer David Cassidy. Shaun's mother is actress Shirley Jones, while David's mother is actress Evelyn Ward. The father of both boys is the late actor Jack Cassidy.

Both Shaun and David starred in a television series prior to having a number-one hit record.

Catch a Falling Star

In March 1958 Perry Como's easy-listening ballad *Catch A Falling Star* received the first Gold Disc Award given by the Recording Industry Association of America (RIAA).

Chad and Jeremy

The duet Chad and Jeremy played a twosome called the Redcoats on an episode of the television series "The Dick Van Dyke Show."

Challenge Records

The West Coast label Challenge Records which produced such hits as *Tequila* by the Champs and *How the Time Flies* by Jerry Wallace, was owned by actor/singer/businessman Gene Autry.

The Champs

In 1957 the Champs had a number-one instrumental hit titled *Tequila*. James Seals and Dash Crofts along with Glen Campbell were later members of that group. Sam Galpin on the session went into a 1970s group named Mallard. Gene Autry named the group the Champs after his movie horse Champion, "The World's Wonder Horse."

Chas Chandler

The manager of the Jimi Hendrix Experience, Chas Chandler, was once a member of the Animals.

Harry Chapin

Tom Chapin, the host of the 1971 television game show "Make A Wish," is the brother of Harry Chapin.

Ray Charles

Ray Charles, born Ray Charles Robinson, changed his name so as not to be confused with the fighter Sugar Ray Robinson.

As a teenager, Ray Charles once played with a white country band called the Florida Playboys. He learned to yodel while playing with the group.

It was Ray Charles who provided the female-sounding backup on his 1959 blues hit *I Believe To My Soul*. He wasn't satisfied with the Raelets sound and overdubbed it himself.

Ray Charles is the only successful artist to have worked in so many different fields of music. A man for all seasons, he is a rhythm-and-blues artist; he has recorded a number of classic jazz albums; his ballads have reached high in the hit charts; his country-western songs have produced two million-selling albums; and his rock 'n' roll records, like *What'd I Say* and *Hit the Road Jack* are some of the best ever produced. He has been in a number of movies, besides singing the theme song for movies such as *In the Heat of the Night* (1967) and the *Cincinnati Kid* (1965).

Chauffeurs

The following artists have at one time served as valets and chauffeurs to other established artists prior to their own success:

Chauffeur	*Artist*
Tyrone Davis	Freddie King
Bobby "Blue" Bland	B. B. King
Larry Williams	Lloyd Price
Billy Swan	Webb Pierce

Chubby Checker

It was Mrs. Dick Clark who thought of the name Chubby Checker, a takeoff on Fats Domino's name.

Chubby Checker married Catharina Lodders, Miss World of 1962.

Cher

Georganna La Pere, Cher's younger sister, is a regular on the television soap "General Hospital."

Cher sang vocal backup on the Ronettes' 1963 Phil Spector production *Be My Baby.* At the time, both she and Sonny Bono were employed by Phil Spector.

Chicago

The members of Chicago made an appearance in the 1973 TV-movie *Electra-Glide in Blue,* starring Robert Blake.

The band Chicago was sued by the Chicago Transit Authority because that is exactly what the group originally called themselves prior to shortening their name to Chicago.

Chicago is the only group to make their record debut with a double album. Titled *Chicago Transit Authority,* it was released in 1969.

In April 1971 Chicago became the first rock group ever to play at New York City's Carnegie Hall.

Chicago saw their first four record albums on the record charts at the same time in 1971.

Chiffons

The female vocal group who sang backup on B. J. Thomas' *Rock and Roll Lullaby* was the Chiffons.

Children

Elijah Blue is the son of Greg and Cher Allman; China (birth certificate reads "god") is the daughter of Grace Slick; Zeke is the son of Neil Young; Mick and Bianca Jagger's daughter is named Jade; Frank Zappa's daughter is named Moon Unit;

Cher and Sonny Bono's daughter is named Chastity while David Bowie's son is named Zowie Bowie; Keith Richard's daughter is Dandelion; Stevie Wonder's daughter is named Aisha Zakiya (Life and Intelligence) and his son is named Kita Swan Di; Billy Swan's son is named Planet; and Ringo Starr's son is named Zak.

Chipmunk Song

David Seville's 1958 novelty record *The Chipmunk Song* received the lowest rating ever on American Bandstand when reviewed by three of the young dancers.

Chordettes

The Chordettes, a female group hailing from Sheboygan, Wisconsin, and discovered by Arthur Godfrey, was the first group to appear on Dick Clark's *American Bandstand.*

Chris and Kathy

Chris Montez and Kathy Young (*A Thousand Stars*) collaborated on a record in 1964 titled *All You Had To Do* (*Was Tell Me*).

Church Bells May Ring

On the 1956 record *Church Bells May Ring* by the Willows, it is Neil Sedaka who is playing the chimes which were later dubbed into the record.

When the record *Church Bells May Ring* was first released on Marty Craft's Melba record label, the song was titled *Church Bells Are Ringing.*

Dave Clark

Prior to becoming a successful singer Dave Clark appeared in movies as either a stunt man or extra. He can be seen being knocked down in a ballroom crowd scene in the 1965 German-British horror film *The Brain*. Dave Clark also appeared in *THE V.I.P.'s* (1963) and *The Victors* (1963).

Gene Clark

Gene Clark of the Byrds was once a member of the New Christy Minstrels.

Michael Clark

Musician Michael Clark was a co-founder of Spirit, Jo Jo Gunne, and Firefall.

Petula Clark

Pet Clark has received gold records for songs sung in English, German, and French. In 1964 alone, she received gold records for *Romeo,* recorded in English; *Monsieur,* recorded in German; and *Chariot,* recorded in French. She recorded her hit *Downtown* in English, Italian, German, and French.

Roy Clark

Singer and guitarist Roy Clark was the first country artist to perform in Moscow and in Monte Carlo.

The Class

In 1959 Chubby Checker cut his first record, which was titled *The Class*. On the label was the statement

"Chubby Checker imitating Fats Domino, The Coasters, Elvis Presley and The Chipmunks."

Claudette

The Everly Brothers' 1958 song *Claudette* ("B" side of *All I Have To Do Is Dream*) was composed by Roy Orbison for his late wife, who was killed in a motorcycle accident.

Patsy Cline

Country great Patsy Cline was the winner on Arthur Godfrey's Talent Scouts on television in 1957 when she sang what was to be her first hit record, *Walkin' After Midnight*. She later appeared as a contestant on Groucho Marx's zany television quiz show "You Bet Your Life."

Patsy Cline perished in a private plane crash, on March 5, 1963, which also took the lives of two other country stars, Lloyd "Cowboy" Copas and Harold "Hawkshaw" Hawkins. The trio was returning from Kansas City, Kansas, where they gave a benefit performance for DJ Cactus Jack Call, who had been killed in an automobile accident. Even then the tragedies didn't end. On his way to the funeral of the plane crash victims, Jack Anglin, the singing partner of Johnny Wright (Johnny and Jack) was killed in an automobile accident on March 7, 1963.

Close To You

Six years prior to the Carpenters' 1970 hit *Close To You,* the song was recorded by Dionne Warwick on her album *Make Way for Dionne Warwick*. The song went nowhere until Karen and Richard Carpenter's recording.

C'mon Everybody

Eddie Cochran's driving 1958 *C'mon Everybody* was originally recorded under the title *Let's Get Together*.

C'mon Everybody was the first rock 'n' roll record ever purchased by Rod Stewart.

The Coasters

Billy Guy and Bobby Nunn, both previous and original members of the Coasters, share the same birthday —June 20, 1936.

Coca-Cola–Pepsi-Cola

Coca-Cola and Pepsi-Cola television jingles have produced two hit records—*I'd Like to Teach the World to Sing* from Coca-Cola, and *Music to Watch Girls By* from Pepsi-Cola.

The Cochran Brothers

Prior to becoming a successful solo artist, Eddie Cochran sang with country singer Hank Cochran as the Cochran Brothers, yet the two were unrelated.

Cozy Cole

In 1958 drummer Cozy Cole had a giant hit with *Topsy Part II*. Although Cozy's name was new to the rock 'n' roll scene, he had previously played with the bands of Benny Goodman, Artie Shaw, Cab Calloway, and Louis Armstrong.

Aaron Collins

The lead singer of both 1950s R&B groups the Cadets and the Jacks, Aaron Collins had two singing sisters who were known as the Teen Queens, a one-hit group that in 1956 gave us *Eddie My Love*.

Judy Collins

As a little girl, Judy Collins was a polio victim, but by the age of twelve she was cured. At age twenty-three she contracted tuberculosis and overcame that also.

Jessi Colter

Singer Jessi Colter has been married to both Duane Eddy and Waylon Jennings.

Come On-a My House

The catchy 1951 hit *Come On-a My House* by Rosemary Clooney was composed by Pulitzer Prize winning author William Saroyan and his cousin Ross Bagdasarian, who would later record under the name David Seville.

Commercial Jingles

There have been a number of songs originating from television commercial jingles, such as *We've Only Just Begun, I'd Like To Teach the World To Sing, No Matter What Shape,* and others. But the music has also flowed the other way. Commercial products have used popular tunes for their commercials. For example: *Feelings* (Pacific Telephone), *Barefootin'* (Spic 'n' Span), *The Candy Man* (M & M Candies), *California Girls* (Clairol Herbal Essence), *That's Life* (Sanyo), *Summertime Summertime* (Ken-L Ration) *Anticipation* (Heinz Catsup), *Calendar Girl* (Purina Cat Chow), *Good Vibrations* (Sunkist), *Tie Me Kangaroo Down, Sport* (Wallaby Squirt), *Mexican Shuffle* (Clark Gum), *Pretty Woman* (Tone Soap), *Close To You* (Hallmark Cards), *Woman* (Enjoli), *Personality* (K-Mart Photos), *Splish Splash* (GTE Flip Phone), *Up, Up and Away* (TWA), *Swingtown* (Ford Mustang), *Hold Me Tight* (Score Hair Cream), *Hot Diggity* (Oscar Meyer), and *Just One Look* (Mazda).

Perry Como

The first rock 'n' roll record made by RCA Victor was Perry Como's cover version of *Ko Ko Mo* recorded in early 1955.

Composers

Here is a partial list of songs composed by well-known performers, but recorded by other artists.

Song	*Recording Artist*	*Composer/ Co-writer*
A Lover's Question	Clyde McPhatter	Brook Benton
A Rainy Night in Georgia	Brook Benton	Tony Joe White
All You Really Want To Do	Cher	Bob Dylan
And I Love Her So	Perry Como	Don McLean
Believe What You Say	Rick Nelson	Johnny Burnette
Both Sides Now	Judy Collins	Joni Mitchell
Crazy	Patsy Cline	Willie Nelson

Song	*Recording Artist*	*Composer/ Co-writer*
Daydream Believer	Monkees	John Stewart
Down in the Boondocks	Billy Joe Royal	Joe South
Dreamin'	Dorsey Burnette	Barry De Vorzon
Dum Dum	Brenda Lee	Jackie DeShannon (c/w)
Early in the Morning	Buddy Holly	Bobby Darin
Emotions	Brenda Lee	Mel Tillis (c/w)
Hello, Mary Lou	Ricky Nelson	Gene Pitney
Hello Walls	Faron Young	Willie Nelson
He's A Rebel	Crystals	Gene Pitney
Hit the Road Jack	Ray Charles	Percy Mayfield
I Feel So Bad	Elvis Presley	Chuck Willis
I Go To Pieces	Peter & Gordon	Del Shannon
I Shot the Sheriff	Eric Clapton	Bob Marley
If I Can't Have You	Yvonne Elliman	Bee Gees
If Not for You	Olivia Newton-John	Bob Dylan
I'm A Believer	Monkees	Neil Diamond
I'm Sorry	Brenda Lee	Ronnie Self
In the Ghetto	Elvis Presley	Mac Davis
It's All Over Now	Rolling Stones	Bobby Womack
It's Late	Ricky Nelson	Dorsey Burnette
Joy To the World	Three Dog Night	Hoyt Axton
Leaving On A Jet Plane	Peter, Paul and Mary	John Denver
Little By Little	Rolling Stones	Gene Pitney
Little Darlin'	Diamonds	Maurice Williams
Lover Please	Clyde McPhatter	Billy Swan
Me and Bobby McGee	Janis Joplin	Kris Kristofferson (c/w)

Song	*Recording Artist*	*Composer/ Co-writer*
Memories of El Monte	Penguins	Frank Zappa
The Mighty Quinn	Manfred Mann	Bob Dylan
Mr. Tambourine Man	Byrds	Bob Dylan
My Guy	Mary Wells	Smokey Robinson
My Way	Frank Sinatra/ Elvis Presley	Paul Anka (c/w)
Needles And Pins	Searchers	Sonny Bono (c/w)
Popsicles and Icicles	Murmaids	David Gates
Quiet Village	Martin Denny	Les Baxter
Reet Petite	Jackie Wilson	Barry Gordy, Jr.
Respect	Aretha Franklin	Otis Redding
Roses Are Red	Bobby Vinton	Paul Evans (c/w)
Ruby Don't Take Your Love to Town	Kenny Rodgers & the First Edition	Mel Tillis
Running Bear	Johnny Preston	J. P. Richardson
San Francisco	Scott McKenzie	John Phillips
She Belongs To Me	Ricky Nelson	Bob Dylan
Stupid Cupid	Connie Francis	Neil Sedaka
Surf City	Jan and Dean	Brian Wilson (c/w)
That's All You Gotta Do	Brenda Lee	Jerry Reed
Turn! Turn! Turn!	Byrds	Pete Seeger
The Twist	Chubby Checker	Hank Ballard
Two Lovers	Mary Wells	Smokey Robinson
Venus In Blue Jeans	Jimmy Clanton	Neil Sedaka (c/w)
When	Kalin Twins	Paul Evans
White Lightning	George Jones	J. P. Richardson

Song	Recording Artist	Composer/ Co-writer
With Pen In Hand	Vicki Carr	Bobby Goldsboro
Wonderful World	Sam Cooke	Herb Alpert (c/w)
Workin' On A Groovy Thing	Fifth Dimension	Neil Sedaka (c/w)
You Beat Me To the Punch	Mary Wells	Smokey Robinson
You Can't Sit Down	Dovells	Dee Clark (c/w)

Carol Connors

Phil Spector was not the only member of the Teddy Bears to go on to bigger and better things. Singer Carol Connors (born Annette Kleinbard) who sang lead on *To Know Him Is to Love Him*, wrote the lyrics for the following movie themes: *Rocky II*, *Looking for Mr. Goodbar*, *The Other Side of Midnight*, plus numerous other films; she also wrote the words for the Rip Chord's 1963 hit *Hey Little Cobra*.

Bert Convy

Actor and television quiz show host Bert Convy was one of the three members of the Cheers, whose one big hit was the 1956 record *Black Denim Trousers and Motorcycle Boots* (written by Mike Stoller and Jerry Leiber).

He recorded the first record ever released on the Era label. It was a rerecording of the 1954 Cheers' song by Leiber and Stoller, *Blueberries*.

Sam Cooke

Sam Cooke sang *Almost in Your Arms* in the 1958 Cary Grant–Sophia Loren movie, *Houseboat.*

The Flamingos' 1960 rocker *Nobody Loves Me Like You Do* was composed by Sam Cooke.

On December 11, 1964, Sam Cooke was shot to death by fifty-five-year-old Bertha Franklin, the manager of the South Figuero Street Motel in Los Angeles.

Sam Cooke was portrayed by Paul Mooney in the 1978 movie *The Buddy Holly Story.*

He was the uncle of singer R. B. Greaves (Ronald Bertrand Greaves), whose biggest release was *Take a Letter, Maria.*

The Cookies

The Beatles' version of *Chains* was actually first introduced by a female group called the Cookies in 1962. The group was formed impromptu when Carole King needed a vocal group to back Little Eva on her number-one hit *Locomotion.*

The Cookies

The Cookies was the female group who backed up Ray Charles on his 1958 hit *Yes Indeed.* The Cookies would later change their name to the Raelets after they left Chuck Willis, whom they had previously backed. This is not the same group that was later organized in 1962.

Rita Coolidge

Rita Coolidge is the daughter of a Baptist minister and the wife of Kris Kristofferson. Rita has a teaching degree and a Master's Degree from Florida State University.

Not only were Eric Clapton and Dave Mason part of Delaney & Bonnie's touring entourage (Friends), but so was Rita Coolidge. She later sang in Joe Cocker's Mad Dogs and Englishmen, before starting a solo career in 1971.

Alice Cooper

Vincent Furnier and his band the Nazz adopted the name Alice Cooper after attending a seance in which a person identifying herself as Alice Cooper talked to the members via a Ouija board.

Alice Cooper filmed an Excedrin television commercial which was never shown.

Alice made an appearance on the television series "The Snoop Sisters."

Alice was elected Homecoming Queen for the University of Houston.

Dave "Baby" Cortez

Piano/organ player Dave "Baby" Cortez, whose biggest hit *The Happy Organ* appeared on the charts in 1959, was previously a singing member of the R&B groups, the Valentines and the Pearls.

The Cosines

Paul Simon and Carole King once recorded demo records under the name the Cosines.

Could It Be Magic

The music for Barry Manilow's composition *Could It Be Magic* is taken from Chopin's *Prelude in C Minor*.

The Country Hams

In 1974 Chet Atkins and Floyd Cramer, with a group called the Country Hams, cut a record titled *Walking In the Park with Eloise*. The Country Hams was an assumed name used by Paul McCartney and Wings. The song was composed by James McCartney, Paul's father.

Country Joe and the Fish

Because of the popularity of Country Joe and the Fish, they were asked to appear on the "Ed Sullivan Show." When it was learned what they planned to sing, the group was paid $10,000 *not* to appear on the program.

Country Wives

Several women have been married to two superstars in country music: Billie Jean Eshlimar was married to both Hank Williams and Johnny Horton. Bonnie Campbell was married to both Buck Owens and Merle Haggard. Sara Davis was married to both Mac Davis and Glen Campbell. Jessi Colter was married to both Duane Eddy and Waylon Jennings.

The Cowsills

The Cowsills provided the theme song music for the television series "Love American Style."

Floyd Cramer

Country pianist Floyd Cramer, whose slip-style became popular in the early 1960s, played piano on Brenda Lee's 1960 ballad *I'm Sorry*.

Crazy Blues

The first record ever made by a black artist was *Crazy Blues*. It was cut in 1920 by Mamie Smith on the Okeh record label.

Crazy Man Crazy

Bill Haley and the Comets' 1953 record *Crazy Man Crazy* was the first rock 'n' roll hit record to make the Billboard chart.

Cream

The group Cream (Ginger Baker, Jack Bruce, Eric Clapton) gave their final performance on November 26, 1969, at the Royal Albert Hall in London.

Creedence Clearwater Revival

Prior to adopting the name Creedence Clearwater Revival, the group had performed under the names the Blue Velvets and the Golliwogs.

Crest Records

In 1956 Eddie Cochran recorded his first single *Skinny Jim* on Crest Records. In 1961 Glen Campbell recorded his first record *Turn Around, Look At Me,* also on the same Crest record label.

The Crickets

The Crickets were the backup band on the Everly Brothers' 1959 hit *Til' I Kissed You.*

On the Buddy Holly recordings, the Crickets never sang; the background vocal was supplied by the two vocal groups the Roses and the Picks.

Jim Croce–Rod Stewart

Jim Croce was born on January 10, 1943, exactly two years prior to the day Rod Stewart was born in 1945.

David Crosby

David Crosby of the Byrds was once a member of bandleader Les Baxter's vocal group, Les Baxter's Balladeers.

Crosby, Stills, Nash and Young

David Crosby, Steven Stills, Graham Nash, and Neil Young began recording together in 1969, forming a group of ex-members of previous groups. Respectively they belonged to: the Byrds, Buffalo Springfield, the Hollies, and again, Buffalo Springfield.

The Cuff Links

The group the Cuff Links, who had three successful releases between 1969 and 1970, was actually Ron Dante who sang all the voices on the records.

Cunningham Brothers

While Bill Cunningham was a member of the Box Tops, his brother B. B. Cunningham was the organist for the Hombres and also the composer of their biggest hit, *Let It All Hang Out.*

Mike Curb

In 1978 Mike Curb was elected Lt. Governor of the State of California. Previously in his early 20s, Curb became president of MGM Records and was the founder of the Mike Curb Congregation.

King Curtis

Sax man King Curtis, whose wailing saxophone could be heard on scores of hits in the 1950s and 1960s (especially on the Coasters' records), was stabbed to death in a fight in New York City on Friday the 13th in 1971.

In the 1978 movie *The Buddy Holly Story,* King Curtis was portrayed by Craig White.

Sonny Curtis

Sonny Curtis, who served as one of the later members of Buddy Holly's band the Crickets, is the singer of the theme song, *Love Is All Around,* for the television series "The Mary Tyler Moore Show."

I Fought the Law, the 1966 hit for The Bobby Fuller Four, was written by Sonny Curtis.

D

The Dakotas

Billy J. Kramer's band, the Dakotas had a hit record of their own in 1963. The instrumental was titled *Cruel Sea* and was released on the Parlophone label.

Dance With Me Henry

In 1955, Etta James recorded a "cleaned-up" version of the R&B hit song *The Wallflower*, retitled *Dance With Me Henry*. The Henry she refers to in the song is meant to be Hank Ballard whose "Annie" records inspired *Dance With Me Henry*. Sung in duet with Richard Berry, the song was such a big hit that the title was used for the 1956 Abbott and Costello movie, *Dance With Me Henry*.

Dandy

The 1966 Herman's Hermits hit *Dandy* was composed by Ray Davies of the Kinks.

Danny and the Juniors

The Philadelphia group Danny and the Juniors first met success when they appeared on American Bandstand to fill in for the scheduled group that failed to appear. They mimed their only record, *At The Hop,* which became an immediate hit.

Ron Dante

Singer Ron Dante's name probably is of little consequence to the average rock buff yet he has been a huge name behind the scenes. Ron Dante dubbed all the voices for the "group" the Detergents, who in 1964 recorded *Leader of the Laundromat* (a takeoff on the Shangri-Las' *The Leader of the Pack*). Ron Dante was also the voices for another group called the Cuff Links. He has produced many records for other artists as well as having sung backup on their recordings.

Bobby Darin

Robert Cassotto chose his professional name by looking through a Bronx telephone book. He got as far as the D's before he stopped at Bobby Darin.

In 1960 Bobby Darin was the youngest performer ever to appear at the Copacabana, until nineteen-year-old Paul Anka performed there later the same year.

Singer Bobby Darin was nominated for Best Supporting Actor in 1963 for the movie *Captain Newman, M.D.*

Erik Darling

Erik Darling has been a member of the Tarriers (along with actor Alan Arkin), the Weavers (he was replaced Pete Seeger), and the Rooftop Singers (*Walk Right In* was their biggest hit).

Clifton Davis

Clifton Davis, star of the television series "That's My Mama," composed the hit song *Never Can Say Goodbye* which was a hit for the Jacksons in 1971.

Dawn

When Tony Orlando began recording for Bell Records (later renamed Arista), his backup vocal group Dawn was comprised of two males. Only later did Dawn become a female duet.

Telma Hopkins, one of the members of Tony Orlando's female duet Dawn, sang as one of the backup singers on Isaac Hayes' hit *Shaft*.

De De Dinah

When Frankie Avalon recorded *De De Dinah* in 1958, he did so holding his nose, as a joke. The novelty sound created his first hit record, taking it to #8 in the United States and #5 in Britain.

Dead Man's Curve

In 1964 Jan and Dean recorded *Dead Man's Curve,* co-written by Brian Wilson. Two years later in 1966, while driving his Corvette, Jan Berry was involved in an automobile accident that left him nearly paralyzed for life. He spent ten months in a coma and suffered some brain damage. The accident occurred near Sunset Boulevard at Whittier Avenue, three blocks from the infamous Dead Man's Curve. In the movie *Dead Man's Curve,* Jan and Dean were portrayed by Richard Hatch and Bruce Davison respectively.

Dear Prudence

The Beatles' song *Dear Prudence* was composed by John Lennon for the sister of actress Mia Farrow.

Dedications

Carly Simon's LP *Anticipation* is dedicated to Cat Stevens. Don MacLean's *American Pie* LP is dedicated to Buddy Holly. Loggins and Messina's album *Sittin' In* is dedicated to Jim Messina's father-in-law, actor Barry Sullivan.

The Del Vikings

At one time there were two groups called the Del Vikings, one recording for Dot Records, the other for Mercury. This came about when the group split up, each side keeping the name Del Vikings. In 1957 each Del Vikings group had a hit record on the charts at the same time—*Whispering Bells* and *Cool Shake.*

Delight

Delight is the Arkansas town where Glen Campbell was born on April 22, 1938.

Delight is the middle name of musician/conductor/composer Quincy Delight Jones.

Delta Lady

When Leon Russell composed *Delta Lady,* he did so for Rita Coolidge.

John Denver

The first host of NBC's "Midnight Special," which debuted August 19, 1972, was John Denver.

John Denver's father, Henry Deutschendorf, Sr., broke a World's Speed Record in a B58 Hustler bomber in 1961.

John Denver once sang with the Chad Mitchell Trio.

Folksinger John Denver was almost signed to play Billy Shears in the 1978 movie *Sgt. Peppers' Lonely Hearts Club Band.* Instead, Peter Frampton was chosen for the role.

Jackie DeShannon

Singer Jackie DeShannon has composed songs recorded by many other artists such as Brenda Lee, the Searchers, and Delaney Bramlett. All in all she has composed over 600 songs, including the theme music for the 1961 movie *Splendor in the Grass.*

Devil Woman

It took British singer Cliff Richard over eighteen years to get a record on the American charts, which he finally did in 1976 with *Devil Woman.*

Barry De Vorzon

Barry De Vorzon, producer of scores for numerous television series such as "S.W.A.T.," had a minor RCA Victor hit record as a teenager in 1957, titled *Barbara Jean.* He also sang lead with the group Barry and the Tamerlanes.

Neil Diamond

The score for the 1973 movie *Jonathan Livingston Seagull* was composed by superstar Neil Diamond.

The Diamonds

In 1957 the Diamonds covered the Rays' version of *Silhouettes* (not surprising, since it was a regular practice in the 1950s for white artists to cover black artists' songs). But in this case the Diamonds went even further when they also covered the Rays' *Daddy Cool* on the flip side, ending up with a two-sided cover.

David Somerville, former lead singer of the Diamonds, sang backup on B. J. Thomas' *Rock and Roll Lullaby.*

Bo Diddley

Bo Diddley's biggest hit record, *Bo Diddley,* was actually an updated version of the old English folk song, *Hush Little Baby.*

Guitarist Bo Diddley played rhythm guitar on two of Chuck Berry's rock songs of the 1950s—*Memphis Tennessee* and *Sweet Little Rock and Roller.*

Different Drum

The Stone Poneys' only hit, *Different Drum,* was composed by Mike Nesmith prior to his becoming a member of the Monkees.

Mark Dinning

Mark Dinning, singer of the famed *Teen Angel* which topped the charts for a while in 1959, is the younger brother of the Dinning Sisters (Ginger Lou and Jean), who in the early 1940s were radio regulars on National Barn Dance.

As a little boy Mark Dinning was sometimes baby-sat by an eleven-year-old girl from down the street named Clara Ann Fowler. Mark's baby-sitter would one day become a recording artist herself, under the name of Patti Page.

Dino, Desi, and Billy

The group Dino, Desi, and Billy was managed by Bill Howard, the son of actress Dorothy Lamour. Dino is the son of actor Dean Martin while Desi is the son of musician Desi Arnaz. The third member of the trio is Billy Hinsche, the brother-in-law of Beach Boy Carl Wilson.

Dion and the Belmonts

Dion's backup group the Belmonts named themselves after the street in the Bronx on which they lived.

Disc Jockeys

Many overnight singing sensations have actually spent years paying their dues. Some singers who spent time as disc jockeys before becoming recording artists were: B. B. King, Bill Haley, James Brown, Jim Lowe, Johnny Tillotson, Rufus Thomas, and Ike Turner.

The Dixie Hummingbirds

The Dixie Hummingbirds won a Grammy Award for the song *Love Me Like a Rock*. Yet they were only the backup group to Paul Simon on the record—a very unusual Grammy.

The daughter of member Ira Tucker, Lynda Lawrence, has sung with both Stevie Wonder's Wonderlove and the Supremes.

Willie Dixon

R&B singer Willie Dixon was a Golden Glove Champion in Chicago in 1936.

Do You Want to Know A Secret?/I Call Your Name

John Lennon and Paul McCartney have composed many songs for other artists and groups, though rarely did the Beatles too record those songs. But after Billy J. Kramer and the Dakotas had hits with *Do You Want To Know a Secret?* and *I Call Your Name,* the Beatles recorded the songs.

Do Your Thing

When the Charles Wright and the Watts 103rd Street Rhythm Band recorded *Do Your Thing,* it was the first time that they had ever sung the song, making up the lyrics as they sang it.

Dr. Hook

The versatile group Dr. Hook and the Medicine Show were fulfilling their own prediction when they appeared on the cover of rock's most prestigious magazine, *Rolling Stone* (March 29, 1973). Earlier in 1973 they had recorded *The Cover of Rolling Stone.*

The band appeared in the 1971 Dustin Hoffman movie *Who Is Harry Kellerman and Why Is He Saying Those Terrible Things About Me?*

Dr. John

Much like actor Humphrey Bogart was the Mellins Baby Food baby, Dr. John (AKA Malcolm John Rebennack) once posed as the Ivory Soap Baby.

Does Your Chewing Gum Lose Its Flavor

In 1961 English folksinger Lonnie Donegan had a hit with the novelty song *Does Your Chewing Gum Lose Its Flavor*. The song was originally composed in 1926 by Billy Rose as the first commercial jingle, originally titled *Does Your Spearmint Lose Its Flavor on the Bedpost Overnight?*

Bill Doggett

Bill Doggett, who in 1956 had the year's biggest hit instrumental with *Honky Tonk,* once played piano for the Ink Spots.

Mickey Dolenz

Mickey Dolenz, ex-member of the Monkees, auditioned for the role of the Fonz just ahead of Henry Winkler, who actually got the part in the television series "Happy Days."

Dolton Records

The very first record released by the small Seattle label Dolton Records became a million seller and reached number one on the charts in 1959. It was titled *Come Softly To Me* by the Fleetwoods (who were named after a telephone exchange, not a model of Cadillac).

Fats Domino

It was Fats Domino who played piano on Lloyd Price's 1952 R&B hit record *Lawdy Miss Clawdy.*

Although Fats has had twenty-two million-seller records on the charts, he has never had a number-one song.

Dominoes

In 1953 when Clyde McPhatter left the R&B group the Dominoes to join the newly formed Drifters he was replaced by a young singer named Jackie Wilson.

Lonnie Donegan

British skiffle singer Lonnie Donegan, who had two U.S. hits with *Rock Island Line* in 1956 and *Does Your Chewing Gum Lose Its Flavor On The Bedpost Overnight?* in 1961, was once a member of Chris Barber's Jazz Band, who had a hit in the U.S. with *Petite Fleur* in 1959.

Donna Reed Show

Both children on the television series "The Donna Reed Show" had hit records in 1962. Paul Peterson, who played Jeff Stone, recorded *She Can't Find Her Keys* while Shelly Fabares, who played Mary Stone, recorded *Johnny Angel.*

Donovan

When the British singer Donovan first came on the scene, he was referred to as the British Dylan.

Don't Let the Sun Go Down On Me

On Elton John's 1975 hit *Don't Let the Sun Go Down On Me,* both Toni Tennille and Daryl Dragon performed on the recording. This was prior to the pair's having their first hit record.

Don't Think Twice It's All Right

Bob Dylan's composition *Don't Think Twice It's All Right* has the same tune as *Who'll Buy Your Chickens When I'm Gone,* an Appalachian folk song discovered by Paul Clayton.

Don't Worry

The unusual sound of a fuzz guitar heard on Marty Robbins' *Don't Worry* came about by accident. The band recorded the song with a broken amplifier, thus introducing the first song to use a fuzz guitar.

Don't You Know

Della Reese's 1959 ballad *Don't You Know* was based on *Musetta's Waltz* from Puccini's *La Bohème.*

The Doobie Brothers

The Doobie Brothers originally called themselves Pud when they first formed in 1970.

Doobie Brothers drummer Tom Johnston once rode with the California motorcycle club the Hells Angels.

Dore

Herb Alpert's son Dore was named after the first two notes on the scale. It was on Dore Records that the Teddy Bears with Phil Spector had the hit *To Know Him Is To Love Him.*

The Dore record label was named after founder John Blair's son Dore.

Lee Dorsey

Prior to Lee Dorsey's recording such hit songs as *Ya Ya* (1961) and *Working In the Coal Mine* (1966), he had been a light-heavyweight contender for the World Boxing Crown, fighting under the ring name of Kid Chocolate.

Dot Records

Randy Wood's phenomenal record label, Dot Records (which actually began as a record order company in Gallatin, Tennessee, in 1951) became one of the most popular labels in the 1950s. One of the company's keys to success was their musical orchestration which was conducted by Billy Vaughn.

In 1955 Randy Wood turned down an offer to buy Elvis Presley's contract from Sun Records for $7500.

Down the Aisle

In 1961 Jimmy Clanton cut an unsuccessful record titled *Down the Aisle,* singing a duet with Miss America of 1959, Mary Ann Mobley.

The Drifters

Solo artist Clyde McPhatter, Ben E. King, and Bobby Hendricks, all with successful solo hit records, were each the lead singer of the Drifters at one time.

In 1958 the entire group was fired by Atlantic Records. Another group called the Crowns was then hired, changing their name and becoming the Drifters. Although it was an entirely new group, the exchange was kept quiet. The lead singer of the new group was Ben E. King.

Drifting Blues

On Charlie Brown's classic recording of *Drifting Blues,* the drummer was Johnny Otis.

Dueling Banjos

Dueling Banjos, the instrumental hit that came from the 1972 movie *Deliverance,* starring Burt Reynolds, was actually composed by Arthur "Guitar Boogie" Smith in the late 1940s as *Feuding Banjos.* Smith had to sue in order to receive royalties for *Dueling Banjos.*

Duets

Here are the real names of some famous rock 'n' roll duets:

Duets	*Real Names*
Billy and Lillie	Billy Ford and Lillie Bryant
Dale and Grace	Dale Houston and Grace Broussard
Dick and Dee Dee	Dick St. John and Dee Dee Sperling
Don and Juan	Roland Trone and Claude Johnson
Flo and Eddie	Mark Bolman and Howard Kaylan
Gallagher and Lyle	Benny Gallagher and Graham Lyle
Ike and Tina	Ike and Tina Turner
Jan and Arnie	Jan Berry and Arnie Ginsberg
(later Jan and Dean)	(Jan Berry and Dean Torrence)

Duets	*Real Names*
Johnnie and Joe	Johnnie Richardson and Joe Rivers
Loggins and Messina	Kenny Loggins and Jim Messina
Marvin and Johnny	Marvin Phillips and Joe Josea
Mickey and Sylvia	Mickey Baker and Sylvia Robinson
Patience and Prudence	Patience and Prudence McIntyre
Paul and Paula	Ray Hildebrand and Jill Jackson
Peaches and Herb	Francine Barker and Herb Feemster
Peter and Gordon	Peter Asher and Gordon Waller
Sam and Dave	Sam Moore and Dave Prater
Shirley and Lee	Shirley Pixley and Leonard Lee
Skip and Flip	Clyde Batton and Gary Paxton

Aynsley Dunbar

Drummer Aynsley Dunbar was a member of the Mojo Men, the Spiders from Mars, the Mothers of Invention, Journey, and currently is with Jefferson Starship.

Bob Dylan

Robert Zimmerman was Bob Dylan's real name, until he had it legally changed in 1967.

In high school Bob Dylan sang with a group called the Golden Chords.

In his youth, Robert Zimmerman spent a short time playing piano for Bobby Vee's group the Strangers, until Vee fired him.

Bob Dylan was once married to *Playboy* bunny Sara Lownds.

In 1963 Bob Dylan was booked to perform on the "Ed Sullivan Show." But when CBS refused to allow him to sing *John Birch Society Talking Blues,* Dylan would not appear on the show.

Bob Dylan played harmonica on Booker T and Priscilla Jones' *Chronicles* album.

E

The Eagles

Some members of the Eagles once served as the backup band for Linda Ronstadt.

Linda Eastman—Yoko Ono

Paul McCartney married Linda Eastman on March 12, 1969. Eight days later John Lennon married Yoko Ono. Linda and Yoko both lived in Scarsdale, New York, and attended Sarah Lawrence College, which was also attended by singers Lesley Gore and Carly Simon.

The Echoes

In 1961 a three man group called the Echoes had only two hit records—*Baby Blue* and *Sad Eyes*. Ironically, in 1974 and 1975 Neil Sedaka would record two of his many self-penned songs. The titles were *Baby Blue* and *Sad Eyes* (same titles, but different songs).

Duane Eddy

The distinct sound of Duane Eddy's guitar can be heard on B. J. Thomas' *Rock and Roll Lullaby*

(1972), and on Nancy Sinatra's *These Boots Are Made for Walking* (1966).

Eight Arms to Hold You

The original title of the Beatles' 1965 movie *Help!* was *Eight Arms to Hold You.* Just prior to the premiere of the film, Capitol Records released the single *A Ticket To Ride* stating on the label "from the United Artists release *Eight Arms to Hold You.*"

El Paso

One of the songs to top the charts in 1959 was Marty Robbins' *El Paso,* the longest number-one song up until that time. Yet the song almost never got released as a single. Columbia Records thought that listeners wouldn't respond to a song that was 5 minutes and 19 seconds in duration. In the 1950s and early 1960s, the average song was about 2 minutes and 20 seconds long.

Eleanor Rigby

Prior to the Beatles' recording the John Lennon–Paul McCartney composition *Eleanor Rigby,* the song was titled *Daisy Hawkins.* (*Daisy Hawkins* would become the title of Stephen Bishop's first recorded song).

The Electric Light Orchestra

Three members of the Electric Light Orchestra played with the London Symphony Orchestra.

The advertisement billboard for the Electric Light Orchestra's *Out of the Blue* album was the most expensive billboard ever built on Sunset Boulevard in Hollywood.

Electricity

Prior to becoming superstars of rock music, the following artists all worked for electrical firms: Elvis Presley, Johnny and Dorsey Burnette worked for Crown Electric in Memphis; George Harrison worked for Blackers in Liverpool; and Paul McCartney worked for Massey and Coggins in Liverpool.

Yvonne Elliman

Yvonne Elliman portrayed Mary Magdalene in the original production of the rock opera *Jesus Christ Superstar*.

The voice of Yvonne Elliman can be heard singing backup on Eric Clapton's 1978 hit *Promises* and on Clapton's previous song *I Shot the Sheriff*.

Elmo Glick

Composers Jerry Leiber and Mike Stoller have written songs under the pseudonym of Elmo Glick.

England Dan

Dan Seals (of England Dan and John Ford Coley) is the brother of Jimmy Seals (of Seals and Crofts).

Ernie and the Heavyweights

Heavyweight boxer Ernie Terrell's rock group was named the Heavyweights. His sister Jean Terrell joined the Supremes when Diana Ross left to sing solo.

Ahmet Ertegun

Ahmet Ertegun, co-founder of one of the most well-respected independent record labels, Atlantic Records, is the son of a Turkish ambassador.

Ahmet Ertegun has composed a number of songs using the name of Nugetre, which is Ertegun spelled backwards.

He is one of the owners of the New York City Cosmos soccer team.

The Essex

The Essex, who in 1963 recorded their first and biggest hit, *Easier Said Than Done,* was formed when all five members, including the two female members, were all in the U.S. Marines.

Paul Evans

Paul Evans, who in 1959 had the novelty hit *Seven Little Girls Sitting in the Back Seat,* is the composer of the Kent cigarette jingle, *Happiness Is.*

The Even Dozen Jug Band

The Even Dozen Jug Band, a group in the mid-1960s, featured such alumni as David Grisman, Steve Katz, Maria Muldaur, and John Sebastian.

Vince Everett

The pseudonym Vince Everett was used for recording by Elvis sound-alike Marvin Benefield. He took the name from the character Elvis Presley played in the 1957 movie *Jailhouse Rock*. In 1963 Vince Everett recorded *Baby Let's Play House* on ABC Paramount Records. Ironically, the three session men on the record were Bill Black, Scotty Moore, and D. J. Fontana, the musicians who originally backed Elvis Presley.

The Everly Brothers

At the height of their careers, in 1962, both Don and Phil Everly quit singing to join the U.S. Marine Corps.

In 1954 the Everly Brothers were hired to perform at a New Orleans nightclub called the Cadillac Club. Owner Louis Brown had just turned down an unknown singer because he had never heard of him, and so instead, he hired the Everly Brothers (who ironically wouldn't have a hit record for another three years). The singer the Everly Brothers replaced was Elvis Presley.

Every Beat of My Heart

Johnny Otis' composition *Every Beat of My Heart* became the first record cut by the Royals (later called Hank Ballard and the Midnighters) in 1952. Nine years later in 1961, *Every Beat of My Heart* became the first record cut by another group—Gladys Knight and the Pips.

Every Beat of My Heart was the only song to occupy two places on the top 100 chart at the same time by the same artist. In May of 1961 *Every Beat of My Heart* by the Pips was in #6 place, while the same song by Gladys Knight and the Pips held #45.

Everyone's Gone To the Moon

The 1965 hit single by Jonathan King, *Everyone's Gone to the Moon,* was recorded by him while he was studying English at Cambridge University.

Everything Is Beautiful

Ray Stevens' 1970 million-seller *Everything Is Beautiful* was the first record released by Andy Williams' Barnaby Record label.

Exodus

The instrumental *Exodus,* theme from the movie of the same name, was a hit for Mantovani, Ferrante and Teicher in 1960, and for Eddie Harris in a jazz mode in 1961.

In 1961 Pat Boone composed lyrics for the song and released a version himself, titling it *The Exodus Song.*

F

Shelley Fabares

Producer Lou Adler's wife Shelley Fabares (niece of actress Nanette Fabray) had a hit record in 1962 titled *Johnny Angel.*

Fabian

In 1973 Fabian Forte posed nude for the centerfold of *Playgirl* magazine.

Fabian was originally considered for the role of Glenn Tyler in the 1961 movie *Wild In The Country*. The role went to Elvis Presley.

The Falcons

In 1959 the Falcons recorded their only successful record, *You're So Fine.* Two later members of the Falcons were Wilson Pickett and Eddie Floyd.

Herb Fame

Herb Fame of Peaches and Herb fame quit show business a few years ago to become a cop in Washington, D. C., but returned to unite with a new Peaches, Linda Greene.

Georgie Fame

Georgie Fame was once the piano player in Billy Fury's backup band, the Blue Flames.

Freddy Fender

Freddy Fender's huge hit *Wasted Days and Wasted Nights* has that 1950s sound for a very good reason, since he originally recorded it in 1959, but it had to wait until 1975 before it became a hit.

Freddy Fender, born Baldemar G. Huerta, spent three years in prison on a marijuana-related conviction. He was arrested on May 13, 1960; it was a Friday.

Fictitious Rock Groups

Herbie and the Heartbeats, from the 1973 movie *American Graffiti* (played by Flash Cadillac and the Continental Kids).

Johnny Casino and the Gambles, from the 1978 movie *Grease* (played by Sha Na Na).

Otis Day and the Knights, from the 1978 movie *Animal House* (played by various musicians).

The Chesterfields, from the 1978 movie *American Hot Wax*. (The Chesterfields were actually offered a recording contract by A & M Records after singing together in the film).

The Fifth Dimension

Two members of the Fifth Dimension (Marilyn McCoo and Florence LaRue) have each held the title of *Miss Bronze*, presented on a television talent show.

The Fireballs

The group that provided the background for the last of Buddy Holly's songs, which were recorded in his home, was the Fireballs. In Norman Petty's studio the Fireballs dubbed their instrumental backing onto the homemade tapes made by Buddy Holly.

First Rock 'n' Roll Hit

Music buffs have argued for years about what was actually the first rock 'n' roll hit record. Here are five chioces which have been mentioned by rock historians:

1. *The Fat Man*	Fats Domino—Imperial—1949
2. *Rocket 88*	Jackie Brenston—Chess—1951
3. *Lawdy Miss Clawdy*	Lloyd Price—Specialty—1952
4. *Crazy Man Crazy*	Bill Haley and the Comets—Essex—1953
5. *Sh-Boom*	The Chords—Cat—1954

Rocket 88 was produced by Sam Phillips, and *Crazy Man Crazy* was the first rock 'n' roll record to make the Billboard charts.

Flaming Star

Elvis Presley's only nonsinging movie was *Flaming Star* (1960), although he does sing the movie's theme song over the credits. (Elvis' role in the film was originally meant for Marlon Brando.)

The Flamingos–The Dells

Johnny Carter was a member of two very popular rhythm and blues vocal groups of the 1950s, the Flamingos and later the Dells.

Mick Fleetwood

Mick Fleetwood is the son of a British Air Force wing commander.

Flo and Eddie

Flo and Eddie were previous members of the Turtles.

Flying Saucer

The original title of Buchanan and Goodman's novelty release *Flying Saucer Part I and II* was *Back to Earth Part I and II.*

Television commentator John Cameron Swazey sued Bill Buchanan and Dickie Goodman for using a character named John Cameron Cameron on *Flying Saucer Part I and II.*

In August 1956 *Flying Saucer* made the rhythm and blues chart, being only the fifth "white" recording to do so.

Flowers In the Rain

Flowers In The Rain, by the Move, was the first song played on BBC's Radio One when it debuted on September 30, 1967.

Foggy Mountain Breakdown

Foggy Mountain Breakdown by Earl Scruggs and Lester Flatt was the theme song of the 1967 movie *Bonnie and Clyde*. The song was originally recorded by the pair back in 1948.

Jim Foglesong

Jim Foglesong, who in the 1950s and 1960s was a backup vocalist for Neil Sedaka and other artists, in 1978 became the president of ABC/Dot Records.

Fool #1

The demo record for Brenda Lee's 1961 *Fool #1* was made by a then unknown singer named Loretta Lynn. Prior to Decca Records selecting the song for Brenda, both Capitol and Columbia Records turned down the demo.

Foolish Heart

The first use of an echo chamber was on Junior Mance's 1950 R&B record *Foolish Heart*. A mike was placed in the bathroom of the Chess Record Studio, thereby creating an echo.

461 Ocean Blvd

461 Ocean Blvd was the Miami house address where Eric Clapton and later the Bee Gees lived. Clapton had one of his albums titled *461 Ocean Blvd*.

For All We Know

Arthur James is the co-author of the 1969 Oscar Winning song *For All We Know* from the 1970 movie *Lovers and Other Strangers*. Arthur James is a pseudonym of David Gates.

For L. P. Fans Only

In 1959 RCA Victor Records released the first album without the artist's name anywhere on the cover, front or back. It was Elvis Presley's *For L. P. Fans Only*. Elvis' picture told his fans all they needed to know.

Fortunes

The British vocal group the Fortunes, whose biggest hit was *You've Got Your Troubles,* recorded the Coca-Cola theme *It's the Real Thing,* heard over American radio and on television.

Four Dates

Although legend has it that Fabian Forte was "discovered" while he was sitting on his front stairs in Philadelphia, he actually sang with an obscure group called the Four Dates in 1958. The group recorded two unsuccessful records prior to Fabian's becoming a solo artist.

Four Preps

Ed Cobb, a former member of the Four Preps, composed the successful songs *Every Little Bit Hurts* and

Dirty Water, recorded respectively by Brenda Holloway and by the Standells.

The Four Seasons

The Four Seasons once recorded two records under the pseudonym the Wonder Who, just for the fun of it. Prior to becoming the Four Seasons (named after a bowling alley), the group had appeared on the "Ed Sullivan Show" as the Four Lovers.

Frankie Valli and the Four Seasons have recorded under a number of names:

Four Lovers	1956
Frankie Vallie and the Romans	1959
Billy Dixon and the Topics	1960
Hal Miller and the Rays	1961
Four Seasons	1962
Frankie Valli and the Four Seasons	1963
Larry and the Legends	1964
Wonder Who	1966

Four Tops

The Motown vocal group the Four Tops have spanned three decades without changing any of the original members.

Kim Fowley

Singer/composer Kim Fowley's father Douglas Fowley portrayed Doc Holliday on the 1955-1961 television series "The Life and Legend of Wyatt Earp." (He was one of two actors who played the role. The other was Myron Healey).

Kim Fowley was previously a member of the novelty group, the Hollywood Argyles.

Peter Frampton

Peter Frampton played guitar on Frankie Valli's recording of *Grease.*

Connie Francis

Connie Francis was a winner on "Arthur Godfrey's Talent Scouts," the television series in the 1950s.

In a court settlement, petite singer Connie Francis was awarded $2,000,000 in damages involving a case in which she was raped on November 8, 1974. In 1979 Connie spoke before a senate committee, pleading for stricter rape laws.

Prior to becoming a hit of the teenage set in 1958 with her first solo hit, *Who's Sorry Now,* she was a singer with the Tommy Dorsey Orchestra.

It was Arthur Godfrey who changed the name of singer/accordionist Concetta Franconero to Connie Francis.

Connie Francis' first million-seller was not *Who's Sorry Now* as is commonly believed. It was in actuality *Majesty Of Love* which she recorded with another MGM Record artist in 1957—Marvin Rainwater.

While a student at Belleville High School in Newark, New Jersey, Connie Francis won the New Jersey State typing contest.

Connie Francis's voice was dubbed in for the singing voice of Jayne Mansfield in the 1959 British movie, *The Sheriff of Fractured Jaw.*

Frankie

Connie Francis' 1959 ballad *Frankie,* which was composed by Neil Sedaka, was dedicated by her to fellow artist Frankie Avalon, whom she had a crush on at the time.

Alan Freed

It is rather ironic that Alan Freed is listed as co-writer on Chuck Berry's *Maybelline* and the Moonglow's *Sincerely,* both being their first hit records. It was one of the benefits of "breaking" their songs on the air.

Although DJ Alan Freed claimed to have coined the term "rock 'n' roll" in the 1950s, a rhythm and blues group named Billy Mathews and the Balladeers recorded a song titled *Rock and Roll,* earlier in 1948.

It was Alan Freed who suggested to John Ramistella that he should change his name to Johnny Rivers, which he did.

Freed was portrayed in the excellent (but chronologically incorrect) 1978 movie *American Hot Wax* by Tim McIntire.

Freight Train

Rusty Draper's 1957 hit *Freight Train* was composed by Elizabeth Cotten at the age of eleven, although the song is credited to Paul Jones and Fred Williams.

Fremont High School

The members of the 1950s R&B groups the Penguins, the Medallions, and the Dootones were all students at Fremont High School in Los Angeles, when they began their recording careers.

Friends

Dave Mason, Bobby Whitlock, Rita Coolidge, Leon Russell, and Duane Allman have all been members of the group Friends at various times.

G

Paul Gadd

Paul Gadd has recorded under the pseudonyms of Gary Glitter, Paul Monday, and Paul Raven.

Garden Party

In 1972 while Rick Nelson was on a bill at Madison Square Garden playing his old standards, he was booed by the audience. The evening so upset Rick that he penned the autobiographical song *Garden Party* to tell about the event. *Garden Party* became a million-seller.

Garfield High

Garfield High is the Seattle, Washington, alma mater of both Quincy Jones and Jimi Hendrix.

Art Garfunkel

Art Garfunkel once wrote under the name Artie Garr. He is a graduate of Columbia University and has an advanced degree in mathematics.

Leif Garrett

Years prior to becoming a popular rock star, Leif Garrett appeared on many television commercials and appeared on the television series "Family Affair" and "Gunsmoke" in bit roles.

Both Leif Garrett and his sister Dawn Lyn appeared in the 1973 movie *Walking Tall*, a biographical film about Sheriff Buford Pusser (Joe Don Baker).

Bob Gaudio

Bob Gaudio, one of the members of the highly successful vocal group the Four Seasons, was once a member of the 1950s group the Royal Teens. It was Gaudio who penned the Royal Teens' biggest hit song, *Short Shorts*.

Bob Gaudio was the producer of the Barbra Streisand–Neil Diamond ballad *You Don't Bring Me Flowers*, Columbia Records' largest selling record.

Marvin Gaye

Marvin Gaye was once a member of the R&B vocal aggregation, the Moonglows.

In 1978 Marvin Gaye filed for bankruptcy, stating he was two million dollars in debt.

Crystal Gayle

Singer Crystal Gayle is the younger sister of country singer Loretta Lynn.

Bobbie Gentry

Singer Bobbie Gentry, who in 1967 had a huge hit with *Ode To Billy Joe,* was born Roberta Streeter. She adopted her last name from the title of the 1952 Charlton Heston movie, *Ruby Gentry.* For a short time, she was married to millionaire gambler William Harrah.

In October 1978 Bobbie Gentry married singer/comedian Jim Stafford.

In order to buy her daughter a piano, Bobbie Gentry's mother traded one of their two cows for a secondhand piano.

Peggy Sue Gerrow

The girl from Lubbock, Texas, for whom the Buddy Holly hit *Peggy Sue* was written was Peggy Sue Gerrow (although he originally considered the song's title as Cindy Lou). Peggy Sue married the Crickets' drummer, Jerry Allison.

Get A Job

If any one song could be blamed for the demise of "Your Hit Parade" on NBC TV, which began on July 10, 1950, it was the Silhouettes' *Get A Job.* When *Get A Job* made the top ten, the program had no choice but to perform the song. Giselle MacKenzie, Snooky Lanson, Dorothy Collins, and Russell Arms, although good singers in their own right, just couldn't handle the yip-yip-yip lyrics.

Joe Namath made his singing debut on the Sha Na Na television show, singing *Get A Job*.

Get Back

The Beatles' *Get Back* was recorded by the four on the rooftop of Apple Records in London.

In hundreds of cases, when a cut is taken off an album and released as a single, the length of the song is reduced. Two examples are the Doors' *Light My Fire* and the Animals' *The House of the Rising Sun,* both of which had less instrumental music on the 45 release. Yet there are exceptions to this rule. For example, when the Beatles' single *Get Back* was released in 1970, it was actually longer than the same cut on their album *Let It Be.*

Andy Gibb

Andy Gibb's first three records made the top of the charts: *I Just Want to be Your Everything* (1977); *Love is Thicker than Water* (1978); and *Shadow Dancing* (1978).

Barry Gibb

Barry Gibb's wife Lynda is a former beauty contest winner, holding the title of Miss Scotland.

Robin Gibb

Robin Gibb was one of the fortunate survivors of one of the worst train wrecks in England's history. While fifty-four people died in the crash and more than a hundred were injured, Robin survived unscathed.

In 1969, Robin Gibb recorded a solo album titled *Robin's Reign.* He came back into the Bee Gees two years later.

Mickey Gilley

Mickey Gilley and Jerry Lee Lewis, who are first cousins, were born within a few months of each other in Faraday, Louisiana.

Mickey Gilley made the *Guinness Book of World Records* when in 1971 he opened Gilley's Club on Spencer Highway in Pasadena, Texas. It is the largest nightclub in the world, with a total capacity of 5,500 people.

Ian Gillian

Ian Gillian, the lead singer of Deep Purple, played the lead of Jesus in the rock opera *Jesus Christ, Superstar.*

The Girl of My Best Friend

Although Elvis Presley was the first to record *The Girl of My Best Friend* which appeared on the album *G. I. Blues,* it was an Elvis sound-alike, Ral Donner, who had the bigger hit with the song in 1961. Both versions of the song sound very much alike.

Go Away Little Girl—Locomotion

Both Steve Lawrence (in 1962) and Donny Osmond (in 1971) have taken their version of *Go Away Little Girl* to the number-one spot on the charts. The only other time this occurred was when *Locomotion* reached the top slot for Little Eva (1962) and again for Grand Funk Railroad (1974). Ironically, in both cases the song was composed by Carole King and her then husband Gerry Goffin.

Andrew Gold

Artist Andrew Gold is the son of composer Ernest Gold and singer Marni Nixon. Ernest Gold has scored many movies, while his wife Marni sang for Deborah Kerr in the movie *The King and I* (1956), for Natalie Wood in the movie *West Side Story* (1961), and for Audrey Hepburn in *My Fair Lady* (1964).

Andrew Gold played guitar on Maria Muldaur's debut album and was a member of Linda Ronstadt's band for two years.

Golden Glove Champions

Jackie Wilson, Willie Dixon, Screamin' Jay Hawkins, Johnny Burnette, and Billy Ward were all Golden Glove Champions in their youth.

Bobby Goldsboro

Pop-country artist Bobby Goldsboro played guitar for Roy Orbison's backup group the Candymen.

Gone

When Ferlin Husky first recorded his biggest hit record *Gone* in 1957, he did so using the name of Terry

Preston. When it was obvious he had a popular hit, his real name was then put on the Capitol Record label.

Good Vibrations

The Beach Boys' 1966 *Good Vibrations* took six months and $40,000 before it was finally put on wax in 1966.

Good Vibrations is the only million-selling Beach Boys single.

Glen Campbell played lead guitar on *Good Vibrations*.

Berry Gordy, Jr.

Founder of Motown Records, producer Berry Gordy, Jr. fought in fifteen Golden Glove fights between 1948 and 1951.

It was Berry Gordy, Jr., who composed Jackie Wilson's first hit record, *Reet Petite,* in 1957.

Singers Harvey Fugua and Marvin Gaye have married Berry Gordy, Jr.'s two sisters, Gwen and Anna respectively.

He became the father-in-law of Jermaine Jackson of the Jacksons, when Jermaine married his daughter Hazel.

Trevor Gordon

Like the Beatles, who started out backing Tony Sheridan on records, the Bee Gees recorded two Barry

Gibb compositions—*House Without Windows/And I'll Be Happy*—behind an unknown singer, credited on the record label as Trevor Gordon and the Bee Gees.

Graham Gouldman

In addition to being the bassist for 10 cc, Graham Gouldman wrote many hit singles for others, including *For Your Love* and *Heart Full of Soul* for the Yardbirds and *Bus Stop* for the Hollies. Gouldman was also a member of the 1960s group, the Mindbenders.

Charlie Gracie

Singer/guitarist Charlie Gracie, who in 1956 had a million-seller with his two-sided hit *Butterfly/Ninety Nine Ways,* had been a contestant two years earlier on the television quiz show "On Your Way," when he was sixteen years old.

Bill Graham

The real name of Berlin-born rock promoter Bill Graham is Wolfgang Wolodia Grajonka.

Grand Funk

The manager of Grand Funk Railroad, John Eastman, is the brother-in-law of Paul McCartney.

Grateful Dead

Grateful Dead founder Phil Leash chose the group's name from an entry in the Oxford Dictionary.

Grease

Grease now holds the record as the longest-running Broadway musical play. The title song for the 1978 movie version was recorded by Frankie Valli. The song did not appear in the play, but was written by Barry Gibb especially for the film version, with Peter Frampton playing lead guitar on the record.

Jerome Green

It is maracas player Jerome Green's voice that can be heard in response to that of Bo Diddley in the 1959 songs *Say Man* and *Say Man, Back Again.*

Greyhound

In 1956 Little Richard composed his first hit record, *Long Tall Sally,* while washing dishes in a Macon, Georgia, Greyhound bus station. In 1968 Tommy Roe composed his hit *Dizzy* while riding a Greyhound bus, and in 1970 Roy Clark recorded *Thank God and Greyhound.* Greyhound Bus Lines was formed in 1913 in Hibbing, Minnesota, the town where Bob Dylan grew up.

Greyhound is also the name of a Jamaican reggae band who once scored in the top ten in Britain.

In the Allman Brothers song *Ramblin' Man,* the singer was born in the backseat of a Greyhound bus on highway 41.

Group Names

The following rock bands named themselves after song titles and lyrics: Jo Jo Gunne, named from the

Chuck Berry song *Jo Jo Gunne;* the Stone Poneys, named after *Stone Poney Blues* by Charley Patton; the McCoys, named from the Ventures' instrumental song *McCoy;* Lovin' Spoonful, named from lyrics of John Hurt's *Coffee Blues;* Skyliners, named from the Charlie Barnette song *Skyliner;* the Pretty Things named after the Bo Diddley song *Pretty Thing;* the Rolling Stones, after Muddy Waters' *Rolling Stone;* Deep Purple, named after the Bing Crosby classic; Fleetwood Mac, from a song of the same name written by Peter Green; and the Doors, from Aldous Huxley's book, *The Doors of Perception.*

Others named themselves after:

Name	*Named After*
Supertramp	*Autobiography of a Supertramp* (1910 book)
Wild Cherry	Cough Drops
Statler Brothers	Tissue Paper
Bachman-Turner Overdrive	Overdrive Magazine
Uriah Heep	Charles Dickens' character (in *David Copperfield*)
Fleetwoods	Telephone Exchange
Procol Harum	Keith Reid's Cat
Bad Company	1972 Jeff Bridges movie
Rufus	Mechanics Illustrated column, "Ask Rufus"

Guess Who?

It was Jesse Belvin's wife Jo Ann who composed the ballad *Guess Who* for her husband, recorded by him just months prior to his death in an automobile accident on February 6, 1960.

On Ivory Joe Hunter's 1959 ballad *Guess Who,* the smooth saxophone of jazz great Johnny Hodges can be heard.

Arthur Gunter

In 1973 blues singer Arthur Gunter won $50,000 in the Michigan State Lottery.

Cornell Gunter

Cornell Gunter has been a member of the Platters, the Flairs, and the Coasters.

H

Sammy Hagar

Sammy Hagar's father was a bantamweight boxer and Golden Gloves Champion. Prior to becoming a musician, Sammy himself took up boxing.

Hale and the Hushabyes

In 1964 *Yes Sir, That's My Baby* was released by Reprise Records, featuring an unknown group called Hale and the Hushabyes. A few of the members of the group were: Sonny and Cher, Jackie DeShannon, Darlene Love, and Brian Wilson. The event was the idea of producer Jack Nitzche.

Bill Haley and the Comets

On the 1950s Decca Records hits of Bill Haley and the Comets such as *Shake Rattle and Roll* and *Rock Around the Clock,* the music was described on the record labels as Fox Trot.

Prior to becoming rock 'n' roll's first group in 1955, Bill Haley and the Comets were a country-western group recording under the name Bill Haley and the Saddlemen.

Scott Halpin

A nineteen-year-old fan named Scott Halpin, who had been in the audience, played drums for the Who in their November 20, 1973 appearance at San Francisco's Cow Palace. Scott played on three songs after the Who's drummer Keith Moon got sick and passed out.

Marvin Hamlisch

Two-time Oscar winner Marvin Hamlisch composed the 1965 Lesley Gore hit *Sunshine, Lollipops and Rainbows.* He's come a long way since.

John Hammond

Columbia record producer John Hammond is credited with the discovery of such well-known artists as Pete Seeger, Count Basie, Billie Holiday, Bessie Smith, Benny Goodman, Aretha Franklin, and Bob Dylan. Bob Dylan in his early years was referred to as "Hammond's Folly."

Lionel Hampton

Bill Doggett, Dino Danelli (a member of Joey Dee and the Starlighters), and Quincy Jones were once members of Lionel Hampton's Band.

The Hanging Tree

Marty Robbins sang the theme song for the 1959 Gary Cooper movie, *The Hanging Tree.* The song was one of the first composed by the team of Burt Bacharach and Hal David.

Tim Hardin

Tim Hardin claims to be a direct descendant of outlaw John Wesley Hardin, whom Bob Dylan incorrectly named an album after in 1969, (*John Wesley Harding*).

The Harlettes

Bette Midler's female vocal backup trio was named the Harlettes. One of the trio's previous members is Melissa Manchester.

George Harrison

George Harrison played lead guitar on Donovan's hit *Sunshine Superman.*

George Harrison was found guilty in 1976 of plagiarizing the 1963 Ronald Mack composition *He's So Fine* for his 1970 hit *My Sweet Lord.*

Freddie Hart

Country singer Freddie Hart taught judo and karate at the Los Angeles Police Academy for two and a half years.

Keef Hartley

When Ringo Starr left Rory Storm and the Hurricanes to join another group called the Beatles, he was replaced by drummer Keef Hartley.

Dan Hartman

Dan Hartman, former bass player for the Edgar Winter Group, and now a solo artist, once had a custom-made jump suit with a bass guitar built in the suit: the cost totaled a little over $5,000.

Harvey Brothers

Les and Alex Harvey have both been accomplished rock musicians. Alex led his own rock band, the Sensational Alex Harvey Band, while brother Les became a member of Stone the Crows.

Bobby Hatfield

Righteous Brothers member Bobby Hatfield once tried out with the Los Angeles Dodgers as a possible future ballplayer.

Donny Hathaway

At age three Donny Hathaway was billed as the nation's youngest gospel singer.

Isaac Hayes

Winner of both the Academy Award and the Grammy Award, Isaac Hayes filed for bankruptcy in December 1976, claiming to be $6,000,000 in debt.

Yusuf Hazziez

Yusuf Hazziez is the Muslim name adopted by R&B singer Joe Tex.

Head

Head (1969) is the only movie in which the Monkees appeared. It was written by Jack Nicholson and Bob Rafelson. Frank Zappa made a cameo appearance in the film.

Bobby Hebb

Both the father and mother of singer Bobby Hebb are blind.

The Hedgehoppers Anonymous

The only successful record by the Hedgehoppers Anonymous was the 1966 novelty release, *It's Good News Week.* In reality, Hedgehoppers Anonymous was Jonathan King.

Help!

The Beatles dedicated their 1965 movie *Help!* to Elias Howe, the inventor of the sewing machine.

Help Me Make It Through the Night

Sammi Smith's 1971 million-seller *Help Me Make It Through the Night,* composed by Kris Kristofferson, was the first record ever released on the Mega Record label.

Help Me Rhonda

Daryl Dragon (The Captain) played organ on the Beach Boys' 1965 hit *Help Me Rhonda.*

Brian Wilson was one of the backup singers on Johnny Rivers' 1975 version of *Help Me Rhonda.*

Jimi Hendrix

Years prior to becoming a superstar, Jimi Hendrix was a musician in the bands of Little Richard, the Isley Brothers, Joey Dee and the Starlighters, and was a member of James Brown's Famous Flames.

Jimi Hendrix once served as a paratrooper in the U.S. Army.

The seven-headed cobra, symbol of the terrorist organization S.L.A., appears on the cover of a Jimi Hendrix album.

The first time Jimi Hendrix set fire to his guitar was at the Old Astoria in Finsbury Park in London in 1966.

Jimi Hendrix once lived in Ringo Starr's flat in Montague Square in London.

He's Got the Whole World in His Hands

One of the first British records to make the American charts was London-born Laurie London's *He's Got the Whole World* (*In His Hands*) in 1958.

Hey Jude

The Beatles' *Hey Jude* was the first single released on the Apple record label (August 30, 1968). It is also the longest number-one song to date (7 minutes, 11 seconds).

Hey Paula

Paul and Paula's 1962 hit *Hey Paula* was originally released via the Fort Worth, Texas, label Le Cam Records. On the label the artists are listed as Jill and Ray (Jill Jackson and Ray Hildebrand). It was only after the larger Phillips Records released the record that the artists' names were changed to Paul and Paula.

Hey There Lonely Girl

Eddie Holman's *Hey There Lonely Girl* was originally recorded by Ruby and the Romantics under the title of *Hey There Lonely Boy*.

(Hey, Won't You Play) Another Somebody Done Somebody Wrong Song

To date the longest title for a number-one record is B. J. Thomas' (*Hey, Won't You Play*) *Another Somebody Done Somebody Wrong Song*.

High School U. S. A.

In 1959 Tommy Facenda recorded a novelty record called *High School U.S.A.* Most listeners were at first shocked to hear their own high mentioned in the lyrics. It is not surprising that so many rock buffs were familiar with the high schools mentioned in the lyrics since Tommy Facenda recorded twenty-eight different versions of the song, distributed across the country.

Tommy Facenda is a previous member of Gene Vincent's Blue Caps.

Gary "U.S. Bonds" Anderson was one of four men who sang vocal backup on Tommy Facenda's original version of *High School U.S.A.* on Legrand Records.

Hillside Singers

Lorri Marsters Ham, a member of the Hillside Singers, is the daughter of musician–producer Al Ham who has been a member of both Artie Shaw's and Glenn Miller's Orchestra. In 1966 he was nominated for an Oscar for the musical score of the movie *Stop the World, I Want to Get Off*.

Al Hirt

Trumpet player Al Hirt was once a judge at a New Orleans high school battle-of-the-bands contest in which a band called the Dominoes won first place. The leader of the group was Dr. John.

Al Hirt was a part-owner of the New Orleans Saints football team.

Al Hirt was once a member of country singer Don Gibson's band.

Hitch Hike

The same vocal backup for Marvin Gaye's version of *Hitch Hike* was later used for the Martha Reeve's version. In fact it was Reeves who sang the backup used on both releases.

Eddie Hodges

Child actor Eddie Hodges, who in 1961 reached #12 on the charts with *I'm Gonna Knock On Your Door*, won $25,000 when he appeared on the television quiz show *"Name That Tune."*

Singer/actor Eddie Hodges appeared in both a Frank Sinatra and an Elvis Presley movie. *A Hole in the Head* (1961) and *Live A Little, Love A Little* (1968), respectively.

Abbie Hoffman

It was Abbie Hoffman whom Peter Townshend of the Who hit over the head with his guitar at Woodstock because Abbie wouldn't get off the stage.

Hold the Line

Toto's 1978 hit song *Hold the Line* was the first 45 RPM picture-disc record.

Buddy Holly

The Beatles and the Rolling Stones have each recorded a song previously made popular by Buddy Holly. The Beatles recorded *Words of Love* while the Stones recorded *Not Fade Away.*

Buddy Holly and the Crickets have never had a number-one record in the United States.

On October 28, 1955, Buddy Holly and Bob Montgomery were the two local musicians who opened a concert in their hometown of Lubbock, Texas. The starring performers on the bill were Marty Robbins and Elvis Presley. Thus, Buddy Holly and Elvis Presley appeared on the same stage in the same evening. In the audience watching the performance was a young lad by the name of Scott Davis, who would one day host his own television series and write songs for Elvis, using the name Mac Davis. This one evening brought together three future superstars; one as a star; another just beginning his career; and the third as yet only a watcher.

On February 2, 1959, at the Surf Ballroom in Clear Lake, Iowa, it was Buddy Holly who played the drums when his fellow artists, Ritchie Valens, the Big Bopper, and Dion performed. This was the last performance for Holly before his death the next day.

Buddy Holly and the Crickets were the first white group ever to play the Apollo Theater in New York in 1957. They were booked because the Apollo thought they were black. The audience accepted these white Texas boys anyway.

Both Buddy Holly (on guitar) and King Curtis (on sax) backed up Waylon Jennings on a 1959 Brunswick release titled *Jole Blon.*

The Hondells

The Hondells were formed by producer Mike Curb in order to record a television motorcycle commercial.

Honey Babe

The 1955 million-dollar *Honey Babe* by Art Mooney and his orchestra was actually composed for the 1955 movie directed by Raoul Walsh, *Battle Cry*.

Honey Cone

Several members of Honey Cone have sung with other groups: Shellie Clark sang with the Ikettes, Carolyn Willis sang with Bob B. Soxx and the Blue Jeans, and Edna Wright was a former Ray Charles' Raelette.

The female trio Honey Cone was formed to sing vocal backup for Andy Williams on his television program in 1969.

John Lee Hooker

Blues singer John Lee Hooker has sung under the pseudonyms of Texas Slim, Delton John, Johnny Williams, and Birmingham Sam.

Nicky Hopkins

Nicky Hopkins has played on sessions with Quicksilver Messenger Service, the Jeff Beck Group, the Rolling Stones, the Who, and the Beatles.

Hotel California

The actual hotel shown on the album cover of the Eagles' *Hotel California* is the Beverly Hills Hotel built in 1912. Nicknamed the Pink Palace, it became a mecca for the stars and starlets of Hollywood.

How Deep Is Your Love

The Bee Gees originally wrote *How Deep Is Your Love* for Yvonne Elliman, but recorded it themselves for the movie *Saturday Night Fever.*

How Do You Do It?

Gerry and the Pacemakers' first hit record *How Do You Do It?,* recorded in 1963, was first offered to, but turned down by, the Beatles. (There does exist, however, a demo of this song by the Beatles).

Engelbert Humperdinck

Engelbert Humperdinck's real name is Gerry Dorsey. He "borrowed" the name from the creator of the opera *Hansel and Gretel.*

Humperdinck was born in Madras, India.

Brian Hyland

Before becoming a known recording artist, Brian Hyland was one of several Elvis soundalikes who were used to cut demo records of new songs for Elvis.

(P. J. Proby was another who recorded demos for Elvis.)

Teenage singer Brian Hyland had his own television series in Argentina, South America, during the 1960s.

I

I Can't Stop Dancing

In 1967 the Houston group Archie Bell and the Drells had a hit called *I Can't Stop Dancing*. Although billed as lead singer on the song, Archie Bell wasn't even present when his group made the record; he was away in Vietnam in the U.S. Army.

I Go To Pieces

Peter and Gordon's 1965 hit *I Go To Pieces* was composed by Del Shannon.

I Love You Ringo

In 1964 Bonnie Jo Mason recorded *I Love You Ringo* on Annette Records in tribute to the Beatles' drummer, Ringo Starr. Bonnie Jo Mason was an assumed name used by Cher Bono.

I Wanna Be Your Man

I Wanna Be Your Man is the only song recorded by both the Beatles and the Rolling Stones. It was composed by John Lennon and Paul McCartney for the Stones.

Ice Station Zebra

Singer Dobie Gray made his film debut in the 1968 movie *Ice Station Zebra,* which was Howard Hughes' favorite movie (he saw it 150 times).

Ida Red

The original title of Chuck Berry's 1956 hit *Maybelline* was *Ida Red.* The name Maybelline was taken from the cosmetic brand name. Berry wrote *Ida Red* as a country song. Prior to Chess Records' recording the song, both Mercury and Capitol Records turned it down.

If Not For You

The 1971 Olivia Newton-John hit *If Not for You* was composed by Bob Dylan for his wife Sarah.

Ike and Tina Turner

Ike and Tina Turner, the soulful duet, have recorded for over fifteen different record labels.

Ikettes

Ike and Tina Turner's three-girl vocal group the Ikettes had a hit record of their own in 1962 with *I'm Blue.*

I'm a Man

Although they are two different songs, the title of the first single recorded by both Bo Diddley and Fabian was *I'm a Man.* When Simon Townshend, the younger brother of Peter Townshend of the Who, recorded his first record, it was titled *When I'm a Man.* One of the first songs composed by Neil Diamond was titled *I'm A Man.*

In 1967 *I'm A Man* was a hit for the Spencer Davis Group (their last).

I'm A Man was the second hit by Chicago and the first for them to make the top 40 (#24).

I'm Easy

When Keith Carridine's rendition of *I'm Easy,* from the 1975 movie *Nashville,* won the Academy Award for Best Song, it was the first country song to win Best Song since the Awards began in 1934.

I'm Leaving It All Up To You

I'm Leaving It All Up To You was the first hit record for Dale and Grace (#1 in 1963), and in 1974 was again a first hit record, but this time for Donnie and Marie. (#4)

I'm So Happy

The first record ever released on Bobby Robinson's Fury record label was *I'm So Happy* by Lewis Lymon and the Teenchords. Lewis Lymon was the brother of Frankie Lymon, who headed the Teenagers.

I'm 10,000 Years Old

One of the worst novelty ideas ever introduced was on the 1971 Elvis Presley album *Elvis Country.* Between the twelve cuts on the album, bits and pieces of Elvis singing *I'm 10,000 Years Old* can be heard.

Impressions

The Impressions, which included lead Curtis Mayfield, were originally the backup group for soul artist "The Iceman" Jerry Butler.

In the Ghetto

When Scott "Mac" Davis composed *In the Ghetto,* he actually titled it *In the Ghetto* (*The Vicious Circle*). In order for RCA Victor to release a 1969 version by Elvis Presley, they obtained permission from Davis to drop the subtitle.

In My Life

Judy Collins' *In My Life* was composed by John Lennon and Paul McCartney.

Irish Rovers

The Irish Rovers, who in 1968 reached #7 in both the United States and Great Britain with their only hit *Unicorn,* had previously made a pilot for a television series with Yvonne DeCarlo about a western saloon keeper who employed an Irish trio.

It Ain't Me Babe

The 1967 million-seller *It Ain't Me Babe* by the Turtles was the very first record ever released on the White Whale label.

It Doesn't Matter Anymore

Ironically, at the time of his death in 1959, Buddy Holly had the song *It Doesn't Matter Anymore* on the charts. The song was composed by an up-and-coming artist named Paul Anka.

It May Be Wrong

In 1959 Frankie Valli recorded a single for Decca records on his slow climb to fame. The company misspelled his name as Frankie Vally, and the ironic title of the record was *It May Be Wrong.*

It's All in the Game

The tune for Tommy Edwards' two-time hit (1951 and again in 1958) *It's All in the Game* was composed by the Vice-President of the United States and a Nobel Peace prizewinner, Charles G. Dawes. Dawes died the very year in which Tommy Edwards introduced the song, 1951.

Itchy Twitchy Feeling

It was the Coasters who backed up Bobby Hendrix on his first hit record *Itchy Twitchy Feeling* in 1958. It was Hendrix's first hit after he left as the lead singer of the Drifters. The Coasters went uncredited on the record label.

J

Jackson Brothers

In 1954 the Jackson Brothers recorded a two-sided flop on Atlantic Records. The record went nowhere, but the two songs did. *Love Me* on the "A" side became a classic for Elvis Presley in 1956, and on the "B" side *Tell Him No* became a hit five years later for Travis and Bob.

Stonewall Jackson

Country singer Stonewall Jackson's real name is Stonewall Jackson, given to him at birth November 6, 1932.

Mick Jagger

In 1970 Mick Jagger appeared in two movies—*Performance* and *Ned Kelly*.

Jefferson Airplane

Jefferson Airplane is the first rock group ever to appear at the Monterey Jazz Festival.

Jennie Lee

Jennie Lee was the Los Angeles stripper who was the inspiration for Jan (Berry) and Arnie (Ginsberg) to compose their 1958 hit record on the small Arwin label, *Jennie Lee.*

Waylon Jennings

Waylon Jennings was once a member of Buddy Holly's group, the Crickets. He gave up his seat to J. P. Richardson on the ill-fated flight that took the life of Buddy Holly, Ritchie Valens, and the Big Bopper (J. P. Richardson).

Buddy Holly bought Waylon Jennings his first bass guitar.

Jim and Ingrid

In the late 1960s Jim Croce and his wife Ingrid recorded an album for Capitol Records titled *Croce.*

Damita Jo

Damita Jo was once a vocalist for Steve Gibson and the Red Caps (one of several groups that recorded *Silhouettes* in 1957).

Billy Joel

Prior to his "overnight" success, Billy Joel played at the Executive Lounge in Los Angeles under the name Bill Martin (Martin being his middle name).

Billy Joel fought in twenty-two amateur boxing matches as a teenager.

Elton John

Elton John, whose real name is Reginald Dwight, took his stage name from the names of two fellow British musicians, Elton Dean and John Baldry. His legal name now is Elton Hercules John.

Elton John won a scholarship to London's Royal Academy of Music for his classical piano playing.

Elton John owns a collection of sunglasses, valued at over $40,000.

It was Elton John who played piano on the Hollies' hit *He Ain't Heavy, He's My Brother*. Elton also appeared on Neil Sedaka's record *Bad Blood*, singing in the chorus, and he can also be heard on Sedaka's *Steppin' Out*.

John Mayall's Bluesbreakers

Some of the members of the British John Mayall's Bluesbreakers were: Eric Clapton, John McVie, Jack Bruce, Peter Green, Mick Taylor, Keef Hartley and Mick Fleetwood. Brian Jones and Charlie Watts were both members of this band prior to joining the Rolling Stones.

Leroy Johnson

Jack Scott was inspired to compose his 1958 hit record *Leroy*, after his friend Leroy Johnson went to jail.

Michael Johnson

Michael Johnson, who in 1978 had a hit with *Bluer than Blue,* was previously a member of the Chad Mitchell Trio.

Norman Johnson

Lead singer Norman Johnson of the group Chairmen of the Board was previously the lead singer of the Showmen, who recorded the classic *It Will Stand* in 1961.

Jonathan Livingston Seagull

Neil Diamond scored the 1973 movie *Jonathan Livingston Seagull,* which was adapted from Richard Bach's best-selling novel.

Booker T. Jones

Organist Booker T. Jones and late artist Maurice White of Earth, Wind and Fire were classmates in grade school in Memphis.

Booker T. Jones' father taught math and science at Memphis' Booker T. Washington High School where Booker attended school. Earlier, Johnny Ace had been a student there.

Brian Jones

Rolling Stones' guitarist Brian Jones once lived in the house that belonged to A. A. Milne, the creator of Winnie the Pooh. (The Canadian group Edward Bear named themselves after Winnie the Pooh's real name, Edward Bear).

Brian Jones passed away on July 3, 1968, exactly three years to the day prior to Jim Morrison's death on July 3, 1971.

Davy Jones

Davy Jones, the smallest member of the Monkees, once played the role of the Artful Dodger in the Broadway version of *Oliver*.

Jack Jones

Like his famous actor/singer father Allen Jones, Jack Jones has become a popular singer; and both have also been married four times.

Quincy Jones

As a teenager, Quincy Jones played in the same band as Ray Charles.

Musician Quincy Jones, who has scored numerous movies and television series, has never driven an automobile.

Quincy Jones provided the music for the television series "The Bill Cosby Show," "Ironside," "Sanford and Son," and the television mini-series, "Roots."

Raymond Jones

Very few people have even heard of Raymond Jones, but he was the young lad who on October 28, 1961, walked into Brian Epstein's NEMS Record Store in Liverpool and requested an obscure record titled *My Bonnie* by the Beatles. The rest, as you know, is history.

Thumper Jones

Country singer George Jones once recorded early rockabilly songs in the 1950s under the pseudonym of Thumper Jones.

Tom Jones

Born Thomas James Woodward, Tom Jones called himself Tommy Scott, and his group was the Playboys (later they became the Senators and finally the Squires). He was renamed after the hero of the Henry Fielding novel *Tom Jones*. Early in his career he was also known as Tiger Tom.

Tom Jones and his wife Linda married one another when each was only sixteen years old.

Tom Jones and actor Richard Burton were both born in the South Wales village of Pontypridd. Burton in 1925, Jones in 1944.

The Journeymen

John Phillips and Scott McKenzie were both members of the same group, the Journeymen.

Just Like Gene Autry: A Foxtrot

On the Moby Grapes album *Wow/Grape Jam*, one of the cuts, titled *Just Like Gene Autry: A Foxtrot*, had to be played at 78 rpm. It proved to be an annoying gimmick.

Just The Way You Are

Billy Joel's Grammy-winning *Just the Way You Are* (Best Record and Song, 1978) was written as a birthday present for his wife Elizabeth in 1977.

Just Walking In the Rain

Johnnie Ray's 1956 hit *Just Walking In The Rain* was originally recorded on Sam Phillips' Sun Record label in Memphis in 1951. It was performed by a group of black singers who formed while in Tennessee State Prison, calling themselves the Prisonaires.

K

Burt Kaempfert

It was Bert Kaempfert who produced the Tony Sheridan Beatles records in Germany on Polydor Records in 1962. In 1960 Kaempfert had his biggest instrumental hit with *Wonderland By Night.*

Kansas City

The original title of Wilbert Harrison's 1959 classic *Kansas City* was *K. C. Lovin'*. The song was the first of many to be composed by Jerry Leiber and Mike Stoller, who were at first accidently credited on the record as Lieber and Stroller.

John Kay

When he was fourteen years old, John Kay of Steppenwolf escaped from East Germany in 1958 under gunfire.

Bob Keene

Record producer Bob Keene holds the distinction of recording the first hit records for both Sam Cooke and Ritchie Valens on his record labels. In 1957

Sam Cooke recorded *You Send Me* on Keene Records, while a year later, Ritchie Valens recorded *Come On Let's Go* on Del-Fi Records. Both record labels were founded by Bob Keene.

Bob Keene cut a record on his own Del-Fi label when in 1960 he recorded *Teen Talk.*

Keep On Dancing

Keep On Dancing was the first charted record by both the Gentrys (#4 in 1965) and the Bay City Rollers (#9 in 1971).

Keith

Born James Barry Keefer, musician Keith in 1968 deserted from the U. S. Army. He was subsequently discharged.

Hubert Ann Kelly

Female member H. A. Kelly of the Hues Corporation was actually named Hubert, after her father.

Killing Me Softly With His Song

The song recorded by Roberta Flack, *Killing Me Softly With His Song,* was inspired while co-composer Lori Leiberman was watching singer Don McLean perform at the Troubadour, in Los Angeles.

B. B. King

Blues singer B. B. King has written jingles for Colgate-Palmolive, Pepsi-Cola, and A.T.& T.

B. B. King claims that his initials B. B. stand for Blues Boy.

B. B. King was once a disc jockey with WDIA in Memphis.

B. B. King–Charlie Byrd

Blues singer B. B. King and jazz guitarist Charlie Byrd were born on the exact same day—September 16, 1925.

B. B. King–Sly Stone

Both B. B. King and Sly Stone were disc jockeys prior to becoming recording artists.

Carole King

Singer/composer Carole King was born the same day the liner *Normandie* caught fire and capsized in New York Harbor—February 9, 1942.

On the Chiffons' 1963 *He's So Fine,* Carole King is the piano player.

Singer/composer Carole King was once married to Charlie Larkey, a member of the Fugs.

Carole King and Gerry Goffin

Here is a partial list of the many hit compositions of the one-time husband and wife team.

Will You Love Me Tomorrow	Shirelles
Go Away Little Girl	Steve Lawrence
Her Royal Majesty	James Darren

Don't Say Nothin' Bad About My Baby	Cookies
Hey Girl	Freddy Scott
One Fine Day	Chiffons
Up On the Roof	Drifters
Locomotion	Little Eva
Take Good Care of My Baby	Bobby Vee

Evelyn "Champagne" King

Soul artist Evelyn "Champagne" King was performing janitorial work at Philadelphia International Records in 1975 when producer Theodore Life heard her singing while she worked. After a period of grooming her voice and style, she successfully recorded her first song, *Shame*.

Freddy King

The valet of blues artist Freddy King became an artist in his own right—Tyrone Davis.

Jonathan King

Singer/producer Jonathan King earned a Master's Degree in English at Cambridge University between 1963 and 1966.

The King Is Gone

Ronnie McDowell's 1977 tribute record to Elvis Presley, *The King Is Gone,* sold a million copies just five days after the record was released.

Don Kirshner

Rock promoter Don Kirshner began in the music field as a co-writer with Bobby Darin in the late 1950s and early 1960s.

Kiss

Kiss members Gene Simmons, Peter Criss, Ace Frehley, and Paul Stanley are never photographed without their show makeup, in order to maintain their privacy. Peter's real last name is Crisscoula, Gene's real last name is Klein, Ace's real first name is Paul, and Paul's real name is Stanley Eisen.

Kiss is probably one of the few rock bands to become comic-book heroes (the Monkees and the Beatles were others). The comic books were unique in that they used the heroes' blood mixed in with the ink on the covers. The comics were released June 30, 1976.

Gene Simmons' tongue measures seven inches, one to two inches longer than a normal male tongue.

The hyping of the group expanded to offspring products such as comic books, pinball machines, and Kiss cosmetics.

Kissin' Time

The first record to make it to the charts for Bobby Rydell was *Kissin' Time*, (#11 in 1959). The first record to make it to the charts for Kiss was *Kissin' Time*, (#83 in 1974).

Larry Knechtel

Larry Knechtel, a member of Bread, has played piano on such classic hits as *Mr. Tambourine Man* by the Byrds (1965); *Classical Gas* by Mason Williams (1968); and *Bridge Over Troubled Waters* by Simon and Garfunkel (1970).

Gladys Knight

Gladys Knight won first place on "Ted Mack's Amateur Hour" on three occasions at age four.

Gladys Knight and the Pips

Gladys Knight and the Pips appeared on the last broadcast of the "Ed Sullivan Show," televised on June 6, 1971.

Knockouts

Former heavyweight champion "Smokin' " Joe Frazier's rock 'n' roll band is called the Knockouts.

Kodachrome

Paul Simon's song *Kodachrome* is a registered trademark. It is shown as such on the record label and album jacket. Because of this fact, it got very little air play on BBC radio in England.

Paul Kossoff

The late guitarist of Free, Paul Kossoff, was the son of British actor David Kossoff.

Billy J. Kramer and the Dakotas

The first four hit songs of Billy J. Kramer and the Dakotas, *Do You Want To Know a Secret, Bad to Me, I'll Keep You Satisfied,* and *From a Window* were penned by John Lennon and Paul McCartney.

Kris Kristofferson

Among all the thousands of rock artists who have recorded a song, talented Kris Kristofferson probably has the most impressive background. Kris is the son of a retired U.S. Air Force major general. In high school Kris was the class president, honor student, and football star. He was a Rhodes Scholar and attended Oxford University. He has authored several books and won first prize in a collegiate short-story contest sponsored by the *Atlantic Monthly.* In school he played football and was a Golden Gloves boxer. In Vietnam he was a helicopter pilot. He was an Army captain and attended flight school, jump school and ranger school. As a civilian, he flew helicopters and served as a janitor at the Nashville Recording Studio. He is a Grammy winner and has appeared in numerous movies, including *A Star Is Born,* playing opposite Barbra Streisand. He has also composed such hit songs as *Me and Bobby McGee* and *Help Me Make It Through the Night.*

L

L. C. Humes High School

L. C. Humes High School is the alma mater of both singers Elvis Presley and Thomas Wayne (of *Tragedy* fame).

Cheryl Ladd

Actress Cheryl Ladd had a hit record in 1978 titled *Think It Over,* reaching #34.

Frankie Laine

Singer Frankie Laine and Ruth Smith once set a marathon-dance record in May 26–October 18, 1932 in Atlantic City, New Jersey, when the couple danced for 145 consecutive days (3,501 hours).

Last Names

Here are the last names for some famous first names:

Anna and the A Train	Anna Rizzo
Booker T. and the MGs	Booker T Jones
Country Joe and the Fish	Joe McDonald
Freddie and the Dreamers	Freddie Gerrity
Gerry and the Pacemakers	Gerry Marsden

Goldie and the Gingerbreads	Goldie Zelkowitz
Harvey and the Moonglows	Harvey Fuqua
Jay and the Americans	Jay Black
Jay and the Techniques	Jay Proctor
Johnny and the Hurricanes	Johnny Paris
Little Anthony and the Imperials	Anthony Gourdine
Little Joe and the Thrillers	Joe Cook
Martha and the Vandellas	Martha Reeves
Rosie and the Originals	Rosie Hamlin
Ruby and the Romantics	Ruby Nash
Shep and the Limelights	James "Shep" Sheppard
Spanky and Our Gang	Elaine "Spanky" McFarlane
Vito and the Salutations	Vito Balsamo
Cher	Cher Bono Allman
Donovan	Donovan Leitch
Dion	Dion Di Mucci
Fabian	Fabian Forte
Little Richard	Richard Penniman
Little Willie John	William Woods
Melanie	Melanie Safka
Meco	Meco Monardo
Oliver	Bill Oliver Swofford
Peter, Paul and Mary	Peter Yarrow, Paul Stookey and Mary Travers

Laverne and Shirley Sing

In 1976 while *Laverne and Shirley* was the hottest television series on the air, Atlantic Records released an album of Penny Marshall and Cindy Williams singing hits of the 1950s. Titled *Laverne and Shirley Sing* the album bombed, selling only 7,776 copies.

Vicki Lawrence

Vicki Lawrence, a regular member on television's "Carol Burnett Show," had a number-one hit record in 1973 with *The Night the Lights Went Out in Georgia.* The song was composed by her then husband Bobby Russell.

Lay Lady Lay

Bob Dylan's composition *Lay Lady Lay* was originally written for the 1969 movie *Midnight Cowboy,* though it was never used. Harry Nilsson's *Everybody's Talkin'* was used instead.

Leaving On A Jet Plane

The Peter, Paul and Mary hit *Leaving On A Jet Plane,* written by John Denver, was originally titled *Babe, I Hate to Go.*

Brenda Lee

Brenda Lee appeared in only one movie, *Two Little Bears,* released in 1962.

Early in Brenda Lee's career, when she sang in Paris' Olympic Theatre, the French newspaper *Le Figaro* ran a front-page story that stated she was in reality a thirty-two-year-old midget.

Legendary Masked Surfers

Bruce Johnson, Terry Melcher (son of Doris Day), and Dean Torrence were the members of the mysterious trio, the Legendary Masked Surfers.

The Legends

In Winter Haven, Florida, a high-school rock band named the Legends had three of its members go on to musical success. Jim Stafford, Kent Lavoie (Lobo), and Gram Parsons.

John Lennon

In 1969, John Lennon became the first recipient of the Rolling Stone "Man of the Year Award."

In March of 1974, John Lennon was thrown out of the Troubadour nightclub in Los Angeles for heckling the performing Smothers Brothers.

John Lennon was sued for plagiarism for his song *Come Together*. It seems that the songs's first two lines are the same as the 1956 Chuck Berry composition *You Can't Catch Me*.

John Winston Lennon legally changed his name to John Ono Lennon.

Here are some John Lennon and Paul McCartney compositions written *for* other artists.

Song	*Artist Who Recorded the Song*
I Wanna Be Your Man	Rolling Stones
A World Without Love	Peter & Gorden

Song	*Artist Who Recorded the Song*
Do You Want To Know A Secret?	Billy J. Kramer & the Dakotas
One and One Is Two	The Strangers
Bad To Me	Billy J. Kramer & the Dakotas
I Call Your Name	Billy J. Kramer & the Dakotas
Tip of My Tongue	Tommy Quickly
Love Of the Loved	Cilla Black
I'll Keep You Satisfied	Billy J. Kramer & the Dakotas
I'm In Love	Fourmost
Hello Little Girl	Fourmost
Like Dreamers Do	Applejacks
From A Window	Billy J. Kramer & the Dakotas
Nobody I Know	Peter & Gordon
I Don't Want To See You Again	Peter & Gordon
That Means A Lot	P. J. Proby
It's For You	Cilla Black
Step Inside Love	Cilla Black
Goodbye	Mary Hopkin

Let It Be

John Lennon and Paul McCartney are the owners of an Academy Award for Best Score in 1971 for the movie *Let It Be.*

Let's Spend Some Time Together

Let's Spend Some Time Together was the title of the song the Rolling Stones sang on their May 2, 1965 appearance on the *Ed Sullivan Show*. It was a "cleaned up" version of *Let's Spend the Night Together*.

Bobby Lewis

It was singer Bobby Lewis of *Tossin' and Turnin'* fame, who helped to pull Jesse Belvin and his wife from their burning automobile in a head-on collision which occurred on February 6, 1960. Jesse Belvin never recovered.

Gary Lewis and the Playboys

Gary Lewis, lead singer of Gary Lewis and the Playboys, is the son of comedian Jerry Lewis. The group's biggest hit, *This Diamond Ring*, was composed by Leon Russell.

Playboys' member Jim West was once a member of the Innocents, the group who backed up Kathy Young on her 1960 recording of *A Thousand Stars*.

Jerry Lee Lewis

While on tour of England, Jerry Lee Lewis, at the peak of his career, decided to marry Myra Brown, his fourteen-year-old cousin. His tour was immediately cancelled and his career immediately took a nose dive.

John Lennon once said that the greatest rock 'n' roll song ever made was Jerry Lee Lewis' *Whole Lotta Shakin' Going On.*

On Jerry Lee Lewis' Sun recordings, including *Whole Lotta Shakin' Going On* and *Great Balls of Fire,* he is credited on the label as Jerry Lee Lewis and His Pumping Piano.

Jerry Lee Lewis was the only guest on television's "American Bandstand" to perform his own songs live instead of lip-syncing as other guests did.

Linda

When composer Jack Lawrence wrote a song about his attorney's little girl Linda Eastman, he titled the song *Linda. Linda* ("I count all the charms about Linda") became a best-selling song in 1947, and the little girl who lent her name to the song grew up to become Mrs. Paul McCartney. In 1962 Jan and Dean recorded their version of *Linda.*

Little Boy Blue and the Blue Boys

Mick Jagger's first musical group in school was Little Boy Blue and the Blue Boys. Dick Taylor, later to become a member of the Pretty Things, belonged to the group.

Little Darlin'

The Diamonds' 1957 hit *Little Darlin'* was originally recorded by the Gladiolas, who featured Maurice Williams as lead singer. It is one of the few instances where the cover version is actually better than the original.

Little Dippers

In 1960, a one-time hit aggregation called the Little Dippers reached high on the charts with the very pretty ballad *Forever*. It was revealed years later that the group was actually the Anita Kerr Singers who have been on hundreds of records singing background vocal.

Little Eva

Eva Boyd was the baby-sitter for married composers Carole King and Gerry Goffin. The pair had "Little Eva" record one of their songs in 1962 on their newly formed Dimension label, and the song, *Locomotion,* immediately became a giant hit.

Little Honda

The Hondells' 1964 hit *Little Honda* was composed by Brian Wilson. It was originally to have been the theme for a television commercial for Honda motorcycles.

Little Red Rooster

On Sam Cooke's 1963 release of the Willie Dixon blues classic *Little Red Rooster,* Ray Charles played piano while Billy Preston played organ.

Little Star

"Twinkle, Twinkle, Little Star," the nursery rhyme on which the Elegants' 1958 hit *Little Star* was based, was composed by Mozart at age five.

Living Doll

The original pressings of British singer Cliff Richard's 1959 hit *Living Doll* actually read by Cliff Richard and the Drifters on the record label. It was at this time that the Drifters changed their name to the Shadows because of the American R & B group the Drifters.

Danny Loggins

The inspiration for the Kenny Loggins' composition *Danny's Song,* which Anne Murray recorded in 1973, was his brother Danny Loggins.

Dave Loggins

Singer Dave Loggins, who in 1974 made the charts with *Please Come to Boston,* is the second cousin of Kenny Loggins.

Julie London

Torch singer Julie London and her composer husband Bobby Troup appeared together on the television series "Emergency." Jack Webb, the show's producer, had been previously married to her.

The Lonely Bull

Herb Alpert's first hit record, *The Lonely Bull,* was originally titled *Twinkle Star* until he visited a bullfight in Tijuana, Mexico, after which he added the Spanish flavor. The song was recorded in his garage.

Lonely Guitar

Annette's 1959 recording of *Lonely Guitar* was composed by Jimmie Dodd, the host of television's "Mickey Mouse Club."

The Longest Day

Teen idols Paul Anka, Tommy Sands, and Fabian, all appeared in the most expensive black-and-white movie ever produced, *The Longest Day* (1962).

Look For A Star

Several versions of the song *Look for a Star* (from the 1960 British movie *Circus of Horrors*) made the charts in 1960. One version was recorded by Garry Miles, an American, and another by a British artist whose name, strangely enough, was Gary Mills (AKA Buzz Cason).

Darlene Love

Darlene Love was a member of several Phil Spector groups. She sang lead on the Crystals' *He's A Rebel,* and later was a member of Bob B. Soxx and the Blue Jeans, who hit in 1962 with *Zip-a-Dee-Doo-*

Dah. She was also the lead singer of the Blossoms who sang backup for Elvis on several records.

She is a sister of Edna Wright of Honey Cone.

Mike Love

Stan Love, the six-foot-nine-inch older brother of Mike Love of the Beach Boys, played basketball for the Baltimore Bullets.

Lonely Surfer

Two of the musicians on Jack Nitzche's 1963 instrumental recording *The Lonely Surfer* were David Gates and Leon Russell.

Love Is Strange

In 1957 Mickey and Sylvia reached the #13 slot on the top 100 with *Love Is Strange.* Ten years later in 1967 Peaches and Herb also reached the #13 slot on the top 100 with *Love Is Strange.*

Love Letters

The piano player of Kitty Lester's 1962 hit *Love Letters* was Lincoln Mayorga, a former member of the Piltdown Men.

Love Me

Love Me, the classic ballad by Elvis Presley, became the only million-seller to make the Billboard charts without being released as a single. The song was composed by the prolific team of Jerry Leiber and Mike Stoller. Prior to Elvis' recording the song, it was recorded by several other artists, including "Her Nibs" Miss Georgia Gibbs.

Love Me Do

The Beatles' first release on the Parlaphone Record label in October, 1962, was *Love Me Do.* It was the first time the Beatles recorded with their newest member, drummer Ringo Starr, yet on this, their first hit record, Ringo played the tambourine, while a studio musician named Andy White played the drums. Andy White is now the drummer for Marlene Dietrich. Andy White played drums on the single version of *Love Me Do,* but Ringo played drums on the version for the Beatles's first album.

Love Me Tender

In 1978 numerous radio stations began playing a song which was a composite of Elvis Presley and Linda Rondstadt singing *Love Me Tender.* Because the composite was never released as a record nor was the tape offered for sale, the radio stations contend that they have the freedom to play any part of any available record they please, making quite a provocative argument.

Love's Made a Fool of You

The Buddy Holly single *Love's Made A Fool of You* was actually cut as a demonstration record for the Everly Brothers in 1959.

The Lovin' Spoonful

The Lovin' Spoonful was the first rock 'n' roll band to play at San Francisco's famed Hungry i.

John Sebastian's band the Lovin' Spoonful backed up Sonny and Cher on their release *They're on the Outside.*

Loving You

In Elvis Presley's 1957 movie *Loving You,* his mother and father (Gladys and Vernon Presley) appear in one scene, sitting in a grandstand as he is singing *Got a Lot of Livin' to Do.*

Lowdown

Boz Scaggs' *Lowdown* was a song that RSO president Al Coury wanted to include on the *Saturday Night Fever* album, which became the best-selling album of all time with twenty-two million copies sold. Scaggs' manager Irv Azoff turned the proposal down, since the song was to be included in the sound track of *Looking for Mr. Goodbar.* Had the song been included, it would have meant one million dollars in royalties for Scaggs.

Jim Lowe

Although *The Green Door* was disc jockey Jim Lowe's only hit record, he had previously composed the Rusty Draper hit *Gambler's Guitar.*

Lucille

B.B. King named his red thirty-dollar Gibson guitar Lucille after he rescued it from a fire started in Twist, Arkansas, by two men who were fighting over a woman named Lucille.

Lucy in the Sky With Diamonds

Although many rock fans claim that the Beatles' *Lucy In the Sky With Diamonds* actually is referring to LSD (initials in the song title), John Lennon claims he got the title from his young son John Julian. The choice is yours.

Donna Ludwig

Donna Ludwig was the girl friend of Ritchie Valens for whom he wrote his classic ballad *Donna.*

Lorna Luft

Judy Garland's daughter Lorna Luft married guitarist Jake Hooker of the group Arrow.

Susie Luke

Susie Luke, the younger sister of composer/singer Robin Luke, was the inspiration for Robin's 1958 million-seller, *Susie Darlin'*.

Lulu

British singer Lulu (co-star of the 1967 movie *To Sir with Love*) is the former wife of Maurice Gibb of the Bee Gees.

Bob Luman

The late country singer Bob Luman, who in 1960 scored his biggest hit with *Let's Think About Living,* turned down a contract to play baseball for the Pittsburgh Pirates.

Peter Lupus

Long before he became Willie Armitage on the long-running television series "Mission Impossible," Peter Lupus, former Mr. Indianapolis and Mr. Hercules, could be seen holding Annette on his shoulders on the cover of the album *Muscle Beach Party.*

Arthur Lyman

Arthur Lyman, who in the early 1960s followed the popularity of Martin Denny's exotic music, recorded one hit record in 1959 titled *Taboo.* Arthur Lyman and his band backed up Connie Stevens in the television series *Hawaiian Eye.*

Arthur Lyman was previously a member of Martin Denny's band.

Cheryl Lynn

Disco artist Cheryl Lynn (*Got to Be Real*) appeared on television's "The Gong Show" in November 1976, singing *You Are So Beautiful.* The judges (Rex Reed, Jaye P. Morgan, and Elke Summer) awarded her the maximum 30 points.

She later played "the Wicked Witch of the West" in the stage version of *The Wiz* in Los Angeles in 1977.

Lynyrd Skynyrd

The rock group Lynyrd Skynyrd was named after the band's high school coach, one Leonard Skinerd.

Group member Ed King was previously a member of the Strawberry Alarm Clock.

The cover of the Lynyrd Skynyrd's last album *Street Survivors* was changed after the deaths of two members of the band, lead singer Ronnie Van Zant and Steve Gaines, in a airplane crash on October 20, 1977. The album cover had originally shown Steve Gaines engulfed in flames.

M

Madame X

When the 45 RPM record was first introduced in 1948 by RCA Victor, it was given the code name of Madame X.

Johnny Maestro

Johnny Maestro was the lead singer for both the Crests and the Brooklyn Bridge.

Taj Mahal

Taj Mahal played the role of Ike in the 1972 movie *Sounder*.

He has a B.A. in Veterinary Science from the University of Massachusetts.

Miriam Makeba

"Click" singer Miriam Makeba married Stokely Carmichael in 1968. She had previously been married to musician Hugh Masekela.

Victor Maltoa

Victor Maltoa was the one-armed drummer with the group, the Barbarians, who had a minor hit in 1965 titled *Are You A Boy Or A Girl.*

Victor Maltoa teaches karate.

Melissa Manchester

Prior to her success as a recording artist, Melissa Manchester appeared on the television soap "Search for Tomorrow" as a singer.

Melissa was once a backup singer for Barry Manilow and Bette Midler.

Her father played with the Metropolitan Opera Orchestra for over twenty years.

Mandy

The original title of Barry Manilow's *Mandy* was *Brandy. Brandy* would later be used as a title for a number-one record for the Looking Glass.

Chuck Mangione

The drummer with Chuck Mangione's band previously played a young lad in the 1967 movie *Cool Hand Luke.*

Barry Manilow

Barry Manilow was once employed as a page boy at CBS.

Prior to becoming a solo artist, Barry Manilow was Bette Midler's arranger.

Barry Manilow is the only living rock artist ever to have five albums on the Billboard charts simultaneously. Ballad singers Frank Sinatra and Johnny Mathis have also had this accomplishment.

On Bette Midler's *Do You Want To Dance,* Barry Manilow played piano.

Prior to become a solo artist Barry Manilow wrote the jingle songs for commercials for State Farm Insurance and Band Aids. He wrote and sang for Stridex and Chevrolet. He sang for Kentucky Fried Chicken, Dr. Pepper, Pepsi-Cola, Jack-in-the-Box and McDonalds.

Mansfield, Ohio

Both the Music Explosion and the Ohio Express hail from Mansfield, Ohio.

Charles Manson

Convicted murderer Charles Manson is alleged to have been a co-composer of one of the Beach Boys' songs, *Never Learn To Love,* released in 1968. Manson supposedly composed the song originally as *Cease to Exist* and turned down any credit on the record.

Marathons

In 1961 a group called the Marathons recorded a minor hit with *Peanut Butter*. Not only did the

Marathons sound a lot like the Olympics, but their song was a takeoff of the Olympic's hit *Hully Gully*. It was later revealed that the group was indeed the Olympics who made a duo hit with basically the same song.

Marketts

In 1962 the Marketts had two instrumental hit records, *Surfer's Stomp* and *Balboa Blue*. The piano player on the records was Leon Russell, while the lead guitarist was Glen Campbell.

Mar-Keys

Stax Record instrumental group the Mar-Keys, whose biggest hit was *Last Night*, was the backup band for numerous artists, including Rufus Thomas on *Walking the Dog*. Isaac Hayes played piano for the studio group for a while. Some of the members of the band departed to form Booker T. and the MGs.

The Marksmen

Boz Scaggs and Steve Miller once belonged to the same high school group, the Marksmen.

Bob Marley

Bob Marley has been presented the Third World Peace Medal on behalf of all the African nations at the United Nations. The award was given by Senegal in July 1978.

Marriages (Past and Present)

James Taylor and Carly Simon
John Maus (of the Walker Brothers) and Kathy Young
Maurice Gibb and Lulu
Kenny Gamble and Dee Dee Sharp
Greg Allman and Cher
Sonny Bono and Cher
Glenn Sutton and Lynn Anderson
Bobby Russell and Vicki Lawrence
Booker T. Jones and Priscilla Coolidge
Kris Kristofferson and Rita Collidge
Waylon Jennings and Jessi Colter
Duane Eddy and Jessi Colter
Bobby Troup and Peggy Lee
Levon Helm and Libby Titus
Steve Lawrence and Eydie Gorme
Tommy Sands and Nancy Sinatra
Phil Spector and Ronnie Bennett (of the Ronettes)
Clarence Carter and Candi Staton
Bill Withers and Denise Nicholas
Neil Young and Carrie Snodgrass
Kenny Rogers and Marianne Gordon (of TV's "Hee Haw")
Quincy Jones and Peggy Lipton
Vic Damone and Pier Angeli
Eddie Fisher and Connie Stevens
Eddie Fisher and Debbie Reynolds
Peter Wolf and Faye Dunaway
Richard Farina and Mimi Baez

Steve Marriott

In 1969 Steve Marriott left the group the Small Faces, which would later feature a singer named Rod Stewart, to establish another group called Humble Pie. Another singer would emerge from this new group, his name being Peter Frampton.

Marshall Tucker Band

The Marshall Tucker Band took their name from the owner of their rehearsal hall.

Ann Martell

It was Ann Martell, wife of folksinger John Denver, who inspired her husband to pen the 1974 hit *Annie's Song*.

Martha and the Vandellas

Martha and the Vandellas backed up Marvin Gaye on his 1962 Tamla Record release *Stubborn Kind of Fellow*. They were not credited on the record at the time since Martha was only a secretary for Motown and the other girls were friends of hers.

Al Martino

Al Martino made his movie debut as a singer (in the style of Frank Sinatra) in the 1972 movie *The Godfather*.

Mashed Potatoes

In 1960 Nat Kendrick and the Swans had a very popular dance record with *Mashed Potatoes*. The group never had a follow-up record under that name, since the real name of the group was James Brown and the Famous Flames.

Barbara Mason

Soulful artist Barbara Mason is the cousin of "Soul Brother Number One," James Brown.

Dave Mason

Guitarist Dave Mason has played on recordings with Deep Feeling, Traffic, the Jimi Hendrix Experience, the Rolling Stones, Friends, and Derek and the Dominoes.

Nick Mason

Nick Mason of Pink Floyd was a schoolmate of Andrew Loog Oldham, the one-time manager of the Rolling Stones.

Johnny Mathis

Johnny Mathis, aside from being a great vocalist, was a track star in high school and San Francisco State College, and at one time had to decide to choose between a career in music and one in sports. He broke the broad jump record at Washington High while setting several track records at college. He was invited to try out for the 1956 Olympics. Fortunately for us, he chose music.

Maybe Baby

The Buddy Holly and the Crickets 1958 hit *Maybe Baby* was co-written by Buddy's mother Mrs. Ella Holley, though she is not credited.

The Crickets recorded *Maybe Baby* in the Officers' Club at Tinker Air Force Base.

Curtis Mayfield–Major Lance

Curtis Mayfield and Major Lance were classmates at Chicago's Wells High School in the 1960s.

George McArdle

Bass guitarist George McArdle quit the popular Australian group the Little River Band to become a minister.

Paul McCartney

Paul McCartney is the sole owner to the rights of Buddy Holly's songs.

Paul and Linda McCartney

Paul and Linda McCartney supplied the theme song for the short-lived 1975 television series "The Zoo Gang."

McCoys

After reaching success with *Hang On Sloopy,* the McCoys had fewer and fewer hits, so the group became the backup band for Johnny Winter.

Jimmy McCracklin

Blues artist Jimmy McCracklin, whose biggest hit was *The Walk* in 1957, was previously a professional boxer who fought in 23 bouts, prior to becoming a singer.

Joe McDonald

Joe McDonald, lead of Country Joe and the Fish, was named by his parents after the Soviet ruler Joseph Stalin.

Mike McGear

Rock artist Mike McGear is the younger brother of Paul McCartney. On his first album in 1974, he was backed by Wings.

Maureen McGovern

In two different years (1972 and 1974), Maureen McGovern recorded a song that she also sang in a movie (*The Poseidon Adventure* in 1972 and *The Towering Inferno* in 1974). Both songs (*The Morning After* and *We May Never Love Like This Again*) won an Oscar, and both songs made the charts. Maureen later had a hit in England with *The Continental,* the first song to win an Academy Award in 1934.

Roger McGuinn

Roger McGuinn of the Byrds once played banjo for the folk group the Limelighters.

Rod McKuen

Poet Rod McKuen was a member of a rock 'n' roll band led by John Saxon in the 1957 movie *Rock, Pretty Baby*.

Ian McLaglan

Musican Ian McLaglan married Kim Moon, the wife of the late drummer of the Who, Keith Moon.

LaMonte McLemore

LaMonte McLemore, a member of the 5th Dimension, previously played professional baseball with the Los Angeles Dodgers' farm club.

Bill Medley

Bill Medley of the Righteous Brothers was originally considered for the role of Jim Bronson in the NBC television series "Then Came Bronson." It was Michael Parks who won the part.

Randy Meisner

Bass guitarist Randy Meisner has been a member of Poco, the Stone Canyon Band, and the Eagles.

Johnny Mento

It was six-foot-five-inch singer Johnny Mento who inspired Jimmy Dean to compose and record his number-one song in 1961, *Big Bad John*.

Freddy Mercury

Singer Freddy Mercury of Queen was born in Zanzibar.

Mercury Records

Quincy Jones became the vice-president of Mercury Records, thus becoming the first black vice-president of a major white record company.

It was with Mercury Records that Helen Reddy won an audition by winning a talent contest in Australia in 1966. But Mercury Records was so uninterested that they wouldn't even let her audition.

Jim Messina

Jim Messina (of Loggins and Messina) is the son-in-law of actor Barry Sullivan.

Bette Midler

Bette Midler once played the minor role of a missionary's wife in the 1966 movie *Hawaii.*

Whenever Bette Midler performs, she insists on being paid in gold rather than by check or in cash.

Bette Midler was named by her mother after screen actress Bette Davis.

The Mighty Quinn

Manfred Mann's 1968 hit *The Mighty Quinn,* composed by Bob Dylan, was originally released as *Quinn the Eskimo.*

The Mike Curb Congregation

Harry Blackstone, Jr. the son of the famous magician, and a magician in his own right, was a member of the vocal group the Mike Curb Congregation.

Buddy Miles

Buddy Miles was the drummer on the 1963 Jaynettes hit (their only one) *Sally, Go 'Round the Roses.*

Roger Miller

In 1965 singer/composer Roger Miller won *five* Grammy Awards.

In 1966 singer/composer Roger Miller won *six* Grammy Awards.

Steve Miller

The person who gave Steve Miller his first guitar and who taught him his first chords was the great Les Paul.

Million-Dollar Session

On December 9, 1956, in the Sun Record studio in Memphis, an event occurred in rock history that became known as the Million-Dollar Session. On that one day, Elvis Presley, Johnny Cash, Carl Perkins, and Jerry Lee Lewis gathered for a jam session on six songs: *Big Boss Man, Blueberry Hill, I Won't Have To Cross the Jordon Alone, Island of Golden Dreams, That Old Rugged Cross* and *Peace In the Valley*. Sun's owner Sam Phillips was there in the studio and taped the session. To this day the tapes have never been released and perhaps never will be.

Ronnie Milsap

On the 1969 Elvis Presley recording of *Don't Cry Daddy,* Elvis sings a duet with the great blind country artist Ronnie Milsap.

Minister's Children

Aretha Franklin, Clyde McPhatter, Alice Cooper, Mark Dinning, Paul Davis, Glen Campbell, Marvin Gaye, Lou Rawls, Sam Cooke, Rita Coolidge, Otis Redding, and Ernie K. Doe are all children of ministers. Jessi Colter's mother is a minister, Curtis Mayfield's grandmother is a church pastor, and both parents of the Pointer Sisters are ordained ministers.

The Miracles

The wife of Robert Rogers of the Miracles is a member of the Marvelettes.

The Miracles' first hit record *Got A Job,* released in March 1958, was the first record made by the group. It was an answer to the Silhouettes' 1957 hit *Get A Job.*

Miss America 1973

Terry Anne Meeuwsen, who won the title of Miss America in 1973, has been a member of the New Christy Minstrels since 1969.

Miss Toni Fisher

The only case where the availability for marriage of a recording artist was given on the record label was in the case of Toni Fisher, whose biggest hit was *The Big Hurt* in 1959. On the Signet Record label she is credited as Miss Toni Fisher.

Mr. Acker Bilk

Acker Bilk learned to play the clarinet while serving in a British Army prison after being convicted of falling asleep while on guard duty.

Acker Bilk's *Stranger On the Shore* became the first British instrumental to top the American charts.

Mr. Lee

The Bobbettes in 1957 had their only hit record with *Mr. Lee;* their follow-up was only a minor entry into the charts tilted *I Shot Mr. Lee.* Mr. Lee was the high school principal at New York City's PS 109, the school the girls attended.

Mr. Tambourine Man

Mr. Tambourine Man, recorded by the Byrds in 1965, is considered by many to have been the first folk-rock hit.

Joni Mitchell

Joni Mitchell painted the cover for the *Crosby, Stills, Nash and Young's Greatest Hits* album.

Mockingbird

Robbie Robertson played guitar while Dr. John played the organ on James Taylor and Carly Simon's 1974 version of *Mockingbird.*

Eddie Money

Eddie Money is a graduate of the New York City Police Academy.

The Monkees

Mike Nesmith and Davy Jones of the Monkees both celebrate December 30th as their birthday.

The Candy Store Prophets were the group that *originally* played and sang for the Monkees on the television series *The Monkees.*

Steven Stills and John Sebastian both auditioned for the group but were turned down.

The Monkey's Uncle

In the 1960s Annette had a minor hit with *The Monkey's Uncle.* The group that backed up her vocal performance was the Beach Boys.

Vaughn Monroe–Bing Crosby–Frank Sinatra

Vaughn Monroe cut a version of the 1954 hit *Black Denim Trousers and Motorcycle Boots,* while years later Bing Crosby recorded the Beatles' *Hey Jude.* Not to be outdone, Frank Sinatra recorded Jim Croce's *Bad, Bad Leroy Brown.*

Monster Mash

One of the musicians on Bobby "Boris" Pickett's 1962 novelty record *Monster Mash* was twenty-one-year-old David Gates.

Moody Blues

The British group the Moody Blues became the first rock band to perform in the People's Republic of China.

Keith Moon

The Who's drummer Keith Moon died on September 7, 1978. September 7th was the birthday of Buddy Holly, which Keith had helped to celebrate with Paul McCartney the night before. Moon passed away in the same apartment in which Mama Cass Elliot died in on July 29, 1974, a flat owned by Harry Nilsson.

The Moonglows

Harvey Fuqua, lead singer of the ballad group Harvey and the Moonglows, is the nephew of Charles Fugua who was a member of the Ink Spots.

Marvin Gaye was once a member of the Moonglows.

The Moonglows later evolved into the successful Spinners.

The Moonglows backed up Bo Diddley on some of his Checker recordings of the 1950s.

Johnny Moore

Johnny Moore sang with both 1950s R&B groups the *5 Royals* and *The Drifters.*

Jim Morrison

Jim Morrison's father was an admiral in the United States Navy.

The late Jim Morrison is buried in the Poets' Corner of the Pere Lachaise Cemetery, Paris, France.

Jim Morrison passed away on July 3, 1971, exactly two years to the day after Brian Jones died, July 3, 1969.

Mousketeers

Five ex-Mousketeers who have entered the recording world are: Johnny Crawford, Annette, Paul Peterson, Dick Dodd, and Cubby O'Brien. O'Brien became the drummer for the Carpenters, and Dick Dodd, the drummer for the Standells.

The Move

The British group the Move was once sued by Prime Minister Harold Wilson because they used an unflattering caricature of him in their advertising.

Movies

In many cases a hit record will come from a successful movie. But in a few cases a movie will develop from a hit record. For example: the Beatles' *Yellow Submarine,* Gerry and the Pacemakers' *Ferry Across the Mersey,* Arlo Guthrie's *Alice's Restaurant,* Bobbie Gentry's *Ode to Billie Joe,* C.W. McCall's *Convoy,* Jeannie C. Riley's *Harper Valley P.T.A., Sergeant Pepper's Lonely Hearts Club Band* by the Beatles, *Who'll Stop the Rain* by Creedence Clearwater Revival, and *Red Headed Stranger* by Willie Nelson, all song titles that became movies.

Mrs. Robinson

Although the song *Mrs. Robinson* by Simon and Garfunkel is associated with the 1967 Dustin Hoffman movie *The Graduate* where it was introduced, only parts of the song are performed in the film and subsequent sound-track album.

Anne Murray

Anne Murray was the first Canadian artist to receive a gold record.

Dee Murray

Dee Murray is the former bassist for the Spencer Davis Group, Elton John, and Alice Cooper.

Murray "The K"–Alan Freed

New York DJ Murray "the K" Kauffman is credited as co-writer of Bobby Darin's first hit single *Splish Splash* in 1958, just as DJ Alan Freed is co-writer on Chuck Berry's *Maybelline.*

Muskrat Love

The Captain and Tennille's *Muskrat Love* was written by Willis Alan Ramsey, who originally titled the song *Muskrat Candlelight.*

My Bonnie

My Bonnie by Tony Sheridan and the Beat Brothers on the Polydor Record label is considered to be the most valuable 45 RPM by record collectors.

The Beat Brothers were actually the Beatles.

(Due to fluctuation in record value prices, a few Elvis Presley records may now be of more value.)

My Boy Lollipop

Rod Stewart played harmonica on Millie Small's #2 hit in both the United States and Britain in 1964, *My Boy Lollipop.*

My Cherie Amour

Stevie Wonder's 1969 hit *My Cherie Amour* was originally titled *Oh My Marcia,* after a former girl friend of Stevie's name Marcia.

My Ding-A-Ling

Recording since 1953, it took Chuck Berry nineteen years before he would get his first gold record in 1972, *My Ding-A-Ling.*

My Eyes Adored You

Only after Motown Records turned down Frankie Valli's recording of *My Eyes Adored You* as "not commercial" did Private Stock Records release the song which went to number one in 1975 in both the United States and Great Britain.

My Girl

The Temptations' 1965 million-seller *My Girl* was written by two members of the Miracles—Ronald White and William "Smokey" Robinson.

My Guy

Mary Wells' biggest hit, *My Guy,* recorded by Motown Records in 1964, was written by Smokey Robinson.

My Own True Love

Jimmy Clanton's 1959 ballad *My Own True Love* is actually lyrics added to the song *Tara's Theme. Tara's Theme* was the recurring theme song of what is probably the greatest motion picture ever produced, *Gone With the Wind* (1939). In 1954 lyricist Mack David added words to Max Steiner's beautiful composition.

N

Johnny Nash

As a nineteen-year-old youth, Johnny Nash appeared in the 1959 movie *Take A Giant Step.*

Nashville Teens

The British group the Nashville Teens, whose only real hit was *Tobacco Road,* began as a backup band for Jerry Lee Lewis and Bo Diddley when both artists toured England.

Needles and Pins

The Searchers' 1964 hit record *Needles and Pins* was composed by Jack Nitzche and Sonny Bono.

Nel Blu Dipinto Di Blu

Domenico Modugno's 1958 hit *Nel Blu Dipinto Di Blu* (AKA *Volare*) became the only Italian record to make number one in the American charts.

Rick Nelson

Ricky Nelson's real first name isn't Ricky, nor is it Rick; it's Eric.

Rick Nelson was once married to Kristin Harmon, the daughter of Michigan football great Tom Harmon.

James Burton, Merle Haggard, and Waylon Jennings have all played guitar backup on Ricky Nelson records.

The New Christy Minstrels

The New Christy Minstrels were originally the vocal group on television's "The Andy Williams Show."

Barry McGuire and Gene Clark are former members of the folk group the New Christy Minstrels, which featured Randy Sparks. Larry Ramos, lead guitarist of the Association, is also a previous member. Bill Zorn, previously with the New Christy Minstrels, formed the New Kingston Trio in 1974, with Roger Gamble and Bob Shane. In the 1960's Kim Carnes was a member. The group made their movie debut in the 1964 movie *Advance to the Rear*. A number of the members of the folk group went on to join Kenny Rogers and the First Edition.

Randy Newman

Movie music composer Alfred Newman, who scored such great films as *The Grapes of Wrath* (1940) and *How the West was Won* (1963), is the uncle of singer Randy Newman.

Olivia Newton-John

Olivia Newton-John is the granddaughter of Cambridge University professor Max Born who won the Nobel Prize in 1954.

At age twelve Olivia won a Hayley Mills look-alike contest.

The sweet-sounding voice heard on John Denver's *Fly Away* is that of Olivia Newton-John.

Olivia Newton-John and country singer Lynn Anderson share the same birthday—September 26, 1947.

Paul Nicholas

Paul Nicholas, who had a superhit in 1977 with *Heaven on the 7th Floor,* has appeared in the Broadway productions of *Jesus Christ Superstar* and *Grease.* In films, Nicholas has appeared in *Stardust* (1975), *Tommy* (1975), and *Sgt. Pepper's Lonely Hearts Club Band* (1978).

Night

Jackie Wilson's powerful 1960 hit song *Night* was based on *My Heart at Thy Sweet Voice* from *Samson and Delilah* by Saint-Saëns.

The Night the Lights Went Out in Georgia

After composing the song *The Night the Lights Went Out in Georgia,* Bobby Russell offered the tune to Cher who turned it down. Russell's wife Vicki Lawrence then recorded the song which went to number one in 1973.

Nilsson

Long before anyone had ever heard of Harry Nilsson, television viewers were hearing his voice in the theme song of the series "The Courtship of Eddie's Father."

He also played Dracula's son in the 1974 movie *Son of Dracula.*

Harry Nilsson has never made a public appearance.

Nitty Gritty Dirt Band

Originally, the Nitty Gritty Dirt Band called themselves the Illegitimate Jug Band.

In 1977 the Nitty Gritty Dirt Band became the first rock band to tour the Soviet Union.

The dirty-looking hillbilly group who appeared in in the 1969 movie *Paint Your Wagon* was the Nitty Gritty Dirt Band.

Richard Nixon

Former President Richard M. Nixon was nominated for a Grammy in 1978 in the "Best Spoken Word" category for the album version of his televised interviews with David Frost.

No Matter What Shape (Your Stomach's In)

In 1965 the instrumental version of an Alka Seltzer commercial was released on Liberty Records, titled *No Matter What Shape.* It was performed by an obscure group called the T-Bones. In reality the group consisted of the trio (Dan) Hamilton, Joe Frank (Carollo), and (Tom) Reynolds.

Nothing New Under the Sun

In 1918, sixty-one years before the Village People had their big hit *Y.M.C.A.*, Irving Berlin composed *In the YMCA*.

Twenty-three years before Crosby, Stills, Nash and Young hit with (*If You Can't Be With the One You Love*) *Love the One You're With*, E. Y. Harburg composed *When I'm Not Near the Girl I Love, I Love the Girl I'm Near*.

O

The Oak Ridge Boys

The vocal backup on Paul Simon's *Slip Slidin' Away* was provided by the Oak Ridge Boys, who have been singing gospel ballads for over twenty years.

Cubby O'Brien–Dick Dodd

Cubby O'Brien and Dick Dodd were both Mouseketeers on the television series "The Mickey Mouse Club." Both became professional drummers, O'Brien with the Carpenters, and Dodd with the Standells.

Odetta

In the 1973 television movie *The Autobiography of Miss Jane Pittman,* folk artist Odetta had a small acting role.

Offering

The Carpenters first album produced by A & M Records was to have been titled *Offering,* but was changed to *Ticket to Ride* when the duo's single entered the charts.

Oh! Neil

In 1959 Neil Sedaka composed and recorded the song *Oh! Carol* about a very close friend named Carole King. A year later in 1960 Carole King returned the compliment by recording a song about her close friend; it was titled *Oh! Neil.*

The O'Jays

The O'Jays, whose original name was the Mascots, named themselves the O'Jays in honor of Cleveland disc jockey Eddie O'Jay (WABQ), who helped them reach success.

Oldies But Goodies

When disc jockey Art Loboe began his label Original Sound Records in 1959, little did he forsee the impact of his project. The label produced a large series of these albums, but due to superstition, excluded Volume 13. *Oldies but Goodies* Volume 14 follows Volume 12.

Old Man Willow

Old Man Willow by Elephant's Memory can be heard as a song played at a private party attended by Dustin Hoffman and Jon Voight in the only X-rated movie to win an Academy Award for Best Picture—*Midnight Cowboy.*

On Broadway

The guitar solo on the Drifters' 1963 hit *On Broadway* was performed by Phil Spector.

One Fine Day

Carole King and Gerry Goffins' 1963 composition *One Fine Day* was originally recorded with Little Eva singing the lead vocal. But the song didn't sound right to the husband and wife composers, so Little Eva's voice was replaced on tape with that of a group called the Chiffons.

One Hit Record, But It Was Number One!

The following is a list of artists who had only *one* hit record in the top 40, but that one release went to the number-one position on the charts.

Little Star (1958)	Elegants
Nel Blu Dipinto Di Blu (1958)	Domenico Modugno
To Know Him Is To Love Him (1958)	Teddy Bears
Purple People Eater (1958)	Sheb Wooley
Teen Angel (1959)	Mark Dinning
Get A Job (1959)	Silhouettes
Alley-Oop (1960)	Hollywood Argyles
Mr. Custer (1960)	Larry Verne
Stay (1960)	Maurice Williams & Zodiacs
Stranger On the Shore (1962)	Mr. Acker Bilk
Hey! Baby (1962)	Bruce Channel
Monster Mash (1962)	Bobby (Boris) Pickett
Telstar (1962)	Tornadoes
Sukiyaki (1963)	Kyu Sakamoto
Dominique (1963)	Singing Nun
Ringo (1964)	Lorne Greene

1001 Ways To Live Without Working

Tuli Kupferberg, the author of *1001 Ways To Live Without Working,* was a member of the Fugs.

Only In America

Jay and the Americans' hit *Only In America* was originally recorded by the Drifters. It was decided not to release the Drifters' version, so Jay and the Americans used the same instrumental track, adding their vocals to the master.

Only You

Prior to the Platters' release of their hit version of *Only You* on Mercury Records in 1956, the group, led by Tony Williams, had previously recorded the song on Cincinnati's Federal label. The first version was nowhere near the clean professional sound of the Mercury release. This can be credited to their newly acquired manager Buck Ram, who cleaned up their sound.

Ooby Dooby

Richard Penner, the composer with Wade Moore of the 1956 Roy Orbison Sun release *Ooby Dooby,* with its juvenile lyrics, is today a Professor of English at the University of Texas.

The original recording of *Ooby Dooby* by the Teen Kings (with Roy Orbison), released on Jewel Records, was the first recording cut at the famous Norman Petty Studios in Clovis, New Mexico.

Roy Orbison

Roy Orbison and Pat Boone attended the same college—North Texas State.

Orbison backed up his friend Pat Boone on his 1954 cover version of *Two Hearts.*

Roy Orbison never performs without wearing sunglasses.

Roy Orbison had the lead role of Johnny Banner in the 1967 Civil War movie, *The Fastest Guitar Alive.*

Orbison is unique in that he toured with both Elvis Presley and the Beatles when both were just beginning their careers.

Original Labels of Hit Records

Song	Artist	Popular Label	Original Label
A Rose and a Baby Ruth	George Hamilton IV	ABC Paramount	Colonial
A Thousand Miles Away	Heartbeats	Rama	Hull
Along Comes Mary	Association	Valiant	Davon
At the Hop	Danny and the Juniors	ABC Paramount	Singular
Baby It's You	Spaniels	Vee Jay	Chance
Bad Girl	Miracles	Motown	Chess
Barbara-Ann	Regents	Gee	Cousins
Book of Love	Monotones	Argo	Mascot

Song	Artist	Popular Label	Original Label
Chantilly Lace	Big Bopper	Mercury	D
Come Go With Me	Del Vikings	Dot	Fee Bee
Come Softly To Me	Fleetwoods	Liberty	Dolton
Earth Angel	Penguins	Mercury	Dootone
Disco Duck	Rick Dees & the Cast of Idiots	RSO	Fretone
Every Beat of My Heart	Gladys Knight and the Pips	Fury	Huntom
The Fool	Sanford Clark	Dot	MCI
For Your Precious Love	Jerry Butler	Vee Jay	Falcon/ Abner
Get A Job	Silhouettes	Ember	Junior
Gloria	Shadows of Knight	Atco	Dunwich
Hanky Panky	Shondells	Roulette	Snap
Happy, Happy Birthday Baby	Tune Weavers	Checker	Casa Grande
Henrietta	Jimmy Dee	Dot	TNT
Hey Baby	Bruce Channel	Smash	LeCam
Hey Paula	Paul & Paula	Philips	LeCam
I Fought the Law	Bobby Fuller	Mustang	Exeter
I Met Him On Sunday	Shirelles	Decca	Tiara
I'm So Lonesome I Could Cry	B. J. Thomas	Scepter	Pace Maker
I'm Stickin' With You	Jimmy Bowen	Roulette	Triple D

Song	Artist	Popular Label	Original Label
In the Still of the Night	Five Satins	Ember	Standord
In the Year 2525	Zager & Evans	RCA Victor	Truth
It's Too Soon To Know	Orioles	Jubilee	Natural
Itsy Bitsy Teenie Weenie Yellow Polka-Dot Bikini	Brian Hyland	Kapp	Leader
Ko Ko Mo	Gene and Eunice	Aladdin	Combo
Long Lonely Nights	Lee Andrews and the Hearts	Chess	Mainline
96 Tears	Question Mark & the Mysterians	Cameo	PA-GO-GO
The Mountain High	Dick and DeeDee	Liberty	Lama
Nite Owl	Dukays	Vee Jay	Nat
One Summer Night	Danleers	Mercury	AMP
Only You	Platters	Mercury	King
Over the Mountain, Across the Sea	Johnnie and Joe	Chess	J & S
Party Doll	Buddy Knox	Roulette	Triple D
Pipeline	Chantays	Dot	Downey
Porterville	Creedence Clearwater Revival	Fantasy	Scorpio
Remember You're Mine	Pat Boone	Dot	Republic

Song	Artist	Popular Label	Original Label
Sea Of Love	Phil Phillips	Mercury	Khourys
Sheila	Tommy Roe	ABC Paramount	Judd
Short Shorts	Royal Teens	ABC Paramount	Power
Signs	Five Man Electrical Band	Lionel	MGM
Silhouettes	Rays	Cameo	XYZ
Susie Darlin'	Robin Luke	Dot	International
Suzie Baby	Bobby Vee	Liberty	Soma
Teardrops	Lee Andrews and the Hearts	Chess	Mainline
That'll Be the Day	Crickets	Brunswick	Decca
There's A Moon Out Tonight	Capris	Old Town	Planet
Walk Don't Run	Ventures	Dolton	Blue Horizon
Wasted Days and Wasted Nights	Freddie Fender	Dot	Duncan
The Way I Want To Touch You	The Captain and Tennille	A & M	Butterscotch Castle
Wipe Out	Surfaris	Dot	DFS
Woo-Hoo	Rock-A-Teens	Roulette	Doran
Wolly Bully	Sam the Sham	MGM	XL
You Cheated	Shields	Dot	Tender
You Talk Too Much	Joe Jones	Roulette	Ric
You're So Fine	Falcons	United Artists	Flick

Tony Orlando

In the early 1960s Tony Orlando appeared on American Bandstand to sing his first hit record *Halfway to Paradise,* a composition by Carole King. Tony made his television debut with his fly open.

Tony Orlando's grandfather played in the official band that welcomed aviator Charles Lindbergh and the Spirit of St. Louis home from France in 1927.

Tony Orlando recorded the demo record of the Carole King/Gerry Goffin composition *Will You Love Me Tomorrow,* which was recorded by the Shirelles.

Orleans

The last band to play at the famed Troubadour Club in Los Angeles was Orleans.

Marie Osmond

Marie Osmond, born Olive Osmond, recorded her first two solo songs in 1973, *Paper Roses* and *My Little Corner of the World,* two songs that had previously been hits for Anita Bryant.

Osmond Brothers

The Osmond Brothers hold the distinction of collecting the most Gold Records (eleven) in a twelvemonth period (1973-1974).

Among the many talents of the Osmond family, composing can be added. The Osmond brothers composed the music for the 1974 movie *Where The Red Fern Grows.*

On the January 24, 1964 broadcast of "Bob Hope Presents the Chrysler Theatre," Mickey Rooney portrayed Eddie Foy while the Osmond brothers played the Seven Little Foys.

Johnny Otis

Johnny Otis claimed to have "discovered" singers Hank Ballard, Jackie Wilson, and Little Willie John, among others. Otis also "claimed" to have written the Leiber/Stoller composition *Hound Dog.*

Our Winter Love

Pianist Bill Pursell's 1963 instrumental hit *Our Winter Love* had previously been released in Canada under the title *Long Island Sound.*

Out of Limits

In 1963 the Marketts recorded an up-tempo version of the theme song of the television series "Outer Limits," titled *Outer Limits.* When the producers of the show threatened a law suit, Warner Brothers changed the title of the record label to *Out of Limits.*

Outlaw Blues

John Oates, of Hall & Oates, had a bit appearance in the 1977 Peter Fonda/Susan Saint James movie *Outlaw Blues,* for which he composed the title song.

P

Jimmy Page

Prior to joining the successful British group the Yardbirds, guitarist Jimmy Page was a musician in the band that backed Engelbert Humperdinck.

On many of the early Kinks' albums, Jimmy Page played guitar.

Jimmy Page played lead guitar on the Tom Jones hit *It's Not Unusual* and Them's hit *Gloria.*

Jimmy Page–John Paul Jones

Jimmy Page and John Paul Jones performed on several of Herman's Hermits' hit records, yet were never part of the group.

Palisades Park

Freddy Cannon's 1962 hit *Palisades Park* was composed by the zany host of television's "The Gong Show," Chuck Barris.

Paris Sisters

The Paris Sisters, who in 1961 scored with their only hit *I Love How You Love Me,* had previously backed Bing Crosby's son, Gary Crosby, on a 1955 Decca release titled *Truly Do His and Hers.*

Parker, Little Junior

Born Herman Parker Jr., it was blues singer Sonny Boy Williamson who nicknamed Herman Junior.

Dolly Parton

Dolly Parton sang backup vocal on Emmy Lou Harris' *When I Stop Dreamin* and on Linda Ronstadt's *I Will Never Marry.*

Dolly Parton is the first female country artist to receive a platinum record award. It was for *Here You Come Again.*

Party Doll–I'm Stickin With You

Two Texas boys named Buddy Knox and Jimmy Bowen composed a couple of songs which they took to an obscure record label called Triple D. The record company released the record with Buddy Knox singing *Party Doll* on one side and Jimmy Bowen singing *I'm Stickin' With You* on the flip. When Roulette Records bought the master they released each side as a single in early 1957 and each became a hit. The Rhythm Orchids were the backup group on both songs.

Gary Paxton

Gary Paxton was once a member of Skip and Flip and later of the Hollywood Argyles.

Peter & Gordon

The British duo Peter Asher and Gordon Waller are both the sons of London physicians.

Peter Frampton Comes Alive!

In 1977 the very first Platinum cassette award was given to the tape of *Frampton Comes Alive!*

Peter, Paul and Mary

The title of the 1967 Peter, Paul and Mary album *Album 1700* was also the Warner Brothers catalogue number.

Colin Peterson

One-time drummer for the Bee Gees, Colin Peterson was previously an Australian child star who had appeared in several movies such as *Smiley* (1957) and *The Scamp* (1957).

Ray Peterson

Ray Peterson, who recorded *Tell Laura I Love Her* (1960) and *Corinna Corinna* (1960), suffered from polio as a child.

Nanker Phelge

Nanker Phelge is the pseudonym used by Mick Jagger and Keith Richard.

Esther Phillips

Little Esther Phillips, born Esther Mae Jones, adopted her last name Phillips after seeing a billboard advertising Phillips Gasoline.

John Phillips

John Phillips of the Mama and the Papas was kicked out of the U. S. Naval Academy at Annapolis.

Pink Floyd

The British group Pink Floyd (originally named Pink Floyd Sound) named themselves for two Georgia blues artists, Pink Anderson and Floyd Council.

Pink Floyd was the first British rock group to use a light show as part of their act.

Gene Pitney

Gene Pitney did not sing the theme song of the 1962 movie *The Man Who Shot Liberty Valance* in the film. It became a hit song for Pitney later, but it was not sung in the film. Actually, the theme song for the movie is titled *Young Mr. Lincoln,* originally used in the 1939 John Ford movie, *Young Mr. Lincoln.*

Gene Pitney composed the Ricky Nelson classic *Hello Mary Lou.* The talented singer also played piano on the Rolling Stones' 1964 record *Little By Little.*

The Platters

The Platters were regular numbers on the "Jonathan Winters Show" on television in 1956.

They were given a contract with Mercury Records in 1955 only because their manager Buck Ram offered them as a throw-in with another group managed by Ram which Mercury wanted to sign up. The group wanted by Mercury was the Penguins, who had a million-selling hit titled *Earth Angel.* The group would never have another hit, but the Platters would have many many million-sellers for Mercury.

Pledging My Love

When Johnny Ace died Christmas Eve, 1954, after an accident in which he was playing Russian roulette, his hit ballad *Pledging My Love* was just climbing the charts. In 1977 when Elvis Presley died and his version of *Way Down* was on the charts, the flip side was *Pledging My Love.*

Pledging My Love by Johnny Ace was the first song which Stevie Wonder ever remembers hearing.

Pointer Sisters

Both parents of the Pointer Sisters are preachers. The Pointer Sisters—Ruth, Antia, Bonnie, and June—sang vocal backup on Chicago's *Skinny Boy.*

Jim Pons

Bass guitarist/singer Jim Pons has been a member of the groups the Leaves, the Turtles, and the Mothers of Invention.

Poor Little Fool

One of Ricky Nelson's best recordings of the 1960s was *Poor Little Fool.* The composer of that classic was Sharon Sheeley, the fiancée of Eddie Cochran, and later the wife of Jimmy O'Neill, host of television's "Shindig" series. Sharon Sheeley was with Eddie Cochran on April 17, 1960, riding in the London taxicab that crashed, killing Cochran and injuring Gene Vincent.

Pops We Love You

Tamla/Motown superstars Diana Ross, Stevie Wonder, Marvin Gaye, and Smokey Robinson recorded the song *Pops We Love You* (1979) in tribute to the father of the founder of Motown Records—Berry Gordy Sr., who died November 21, 1978.

Portrayals

The following artists have been portrayed in either the movies or on television:

Artist	*Actor*	*Movie*
Buddy Holly	Gary Busey	*The Buddy Holly Story* (1978)
Crickets	Don Stroud and Charlie Martin Smith	*The Buddy Holly Story* (1978)
Elvis Presley	Kurt Russell	*Elvis* (1979)
Janis Joplin (loosely)	Bette Midler	*The Rose* (1979)
Eddie Cochran	Jerry Zaremba	*The Buddy Holly Story* (1978)
Big Bopper	Gailard Sartain	*The Buddy Holly Story* (1978)
Jan Berry	Richard Hatch	*Deadman's Curve* (1978) TV
Dean Torrence	Bruce Davison	*Deadman's Curve* (1978) TV
Alan Freed	Tim McIntire	*American Hot Wax* (1978)

Artist	*Actor*	*Movie*
Frank Sinatra (loosely)	Al Martino	*The Godfather*
Leadbelly	Paul Benjamin	*Leadbelly* (1976)
Hank Williams	George Hamilton	*Your Cheatin' Heart* (1964)
Woody Guthrie	David Carradine	*Bound for Glory* (1977)
Frank Zappa	Ringo Starr	*200 Motels* (1971)
Sam Cooke	Paul Mooney	*The Buddy Holly Story* (1978)
Ritchie Valens	Gilbert Meigar	*The Buddy Holly Story* (1978)
Jefferson "Blind" Lemon	Art Evans	*Leadbelly* (1976)
Carole King (loosely)	Laraine Newman	*American Hot Wax* (1978)

Sandy Posey–Martha Reeves–Minnie Riperton

Prior to becoming recording artists, both Sandy Posey and Martha Reeves were employed as secretaries for the studios in which they each were discovered. Minnie Riperton worked at Chess Records as a receptionist.

Elvis Presley

In 1955 Sam Phillips, head of Sun Records, attempted to sell Elvis Presley's contract to Randy Wood of Dot Records for $7500. Wood turned down Phillips' offer since he already had an up-and-coming artist under contract—a youngster named Eugene "Pat" Boone whom he had just acquired from Republic Records of Nashville.

Three weeks following the death of Elvis Presley, fifteen of his albums were among the top 100.

According to an FBI memo written by an agent, Elvis Presley once volunteered in 1970 to become an informant for the agency because he didn't like the influence of the Beatles and other groups.

In 1954 Elvis Presley paid $4.00 at the Memphis Recording Studio to record two songs. Those two cuts were *My Happiness* and *That's When Your Heartaches Begin.*

In the 1957 movie *Jailhouse Rock,* Elvis Presley played a singing prisoner named Vince Everett. The following year an unknown Elvis sound-alike named Marvin Benefield cut several records under the pseudonym of Vince Everett. His first release was *Baby Let's Play House* which was backed by Bill Black, Scotty Moore and D. J. Fontana. The three musicians had previously been Elvis Presley's original backup band, called the Blue Moon Boys.

Billy Preston

Billy Preston's mother, Ernesta Wade, played the Kingfish's wife Sapphire on both the radio and television series "Amos 'n' Andy."

Years before he would be a successful artist, ten-year-old Billy Preston played a bit part in the 1958 movie *St. Louis Blues,* the biographical movie of W. C. Handy.

Billy Preston was the first artist other than the Beatles to be credited on a Beatles' record.

Previous Group Names

Current Name	*Previous Name(s)*
Allman Brothers	Hourglass
Ambrosia	Sentrys
American Breed	Gary and the Nitelites
Angels	Blue Angels/Starlite
Association	Men
Average White Band	Stone the Crows
Bachman-Turner Overdrive	Brave Belt
Badfinger	Iveys
Bay City Rollers	Saxons
Beach Boys	Pendletons/Kenny and the Cadets/Carl and the Passions
Beatles	Quarrymen/Johnny and the Moondogs/Silver Beatles
Beau Brummels	Irish Americans
Bee Gees	Blue Cats
Belmonts	Tamarlanes
Bill Haley and the Comets	Bill Haley's Saddlemen
Billy J. Kramer and the Dakotas	Billy J. Kramer and the Coasters
Black Sabbath	Earth
Bloodstone	Sinceres
Bread	Pleasure Faire
Byrds	Beefeaters/Jet Set
Cadillacs	Carnations
Carpenters	Spectrum
Chic	Big Apple Band
Chicago	Big Thing

Current Name	*Previous Name(s)*
Chiffons	Sweethearts
Chi-Lites	Hi-Lites
Cleftones	Silvertones
Commodores	Jays
Crazy Horse	Rockets/Cyrcle
Creedence Clearwater Revival	Blue Velvets/Golliwogs
Crickets	Three Tunes
Crusaders	Modern Jazz Sextet
Cyrkle	Rhodells
Danny and the Juniors	Juvenairs
Delfonics	Harts
Dells	El Rays
Dion and the Belmonts	Dion and the Timberlanes
Doobie Brothers	Pud
Doors	Psychedelic Rangers
Dovells	Cashmeres
Eagles	Teen King and the Emergencies
Earth Band	Chapter Three
Edison Lighthouse	Greenfield Hammer
Edwin Hawkins Singers	Northern California State Youth Choir
El Dorados	Five Stars
Fifth Dimension	Versatiles/Vocals
Five Keys	Sentimental Four
Five Satins	Scarlets
Fleetwoods	Two Girls and a Guy
Four Seasons	Variations/Four Lovers
Four Tops	Four Aims
Freddie and the Dreamers	Red Sox

Current Name	*Previous Name(s)*
Gladiolas	Royal Charms
Gladys Knight and the Pips	Premiers
Grand Funk Railroad	Terry Knight and the Pack
Grass Roots	Thirteenth Floor
Grateful Dead	Warlocks/Hart Valley Drifters
Guess Who	Chad Allen and the Reflections
Hank Ballard and the Midniters	Royals
Heart	White Heart
Herman's Hermits	Heartbeats
Hollies	Deltas/Fortunes
Hudson Brothers	New Yorkers
Impressions	Roosters
J. Geils Band	Hallucinations
Kansas	White Clover/Gimlets
Kinks	Ravens
Kiss	Bullfrog Bheer
Jan and Dean	Barons
L.T.D.	Lovemen
Little Caesar and the Romans	Up-Fronts
Little River Band	Mississippi
Lost Planet Airmen	Fantasy Surfing Beavers
Main Ingredient	Poets
Mamas and the Papas	Mugwumps
Manfred Mann	Mann-Hugg Blues Brothers
Manhattans	Dulcets
Marmalade	Gaylords

Current Name	*Previous Name(s)*
McCoys	Rick Z. Combo/Rick & the Raiders
Moonglows	Crazy Sounds
Mothers of Invention	Soul Giants
Mungo Jerry	Good Earth Rock & Roll
New Christy Minstrels	Virginia Serenaders
Ohio Players	Ohio Untouchables
O'Jays	Mascots
Ozark Mountain Daredevils	Buffalo Chips
Patti LaBelle and the Bluebelles	Sweethearts of the Apollo
Paul Revere and the Raiders	Downbeats
Playmates	Nitwits
Poco	Pogo
Queen	Smile
Rare Earth	Sunliners
Raspberries	Choir
Rolling Stones	Silver Rolling Stones
Ronettes	Ronnie and the Relatives
Rufus	Ask Rufus/American Bread/Smoke
Sandpipers	Grads
Seeds	Ameoba
Shangri-Las	Bon Bons
Silhouettes	Gospel Tornadoes
Sir Douglas Quintet	Doug Sahm and the MarKays
Six Teens	Sweeteens
Skyliners	Crescents

Current Name	*Previous Name(s)*
Sonny Til and the Orioles	Vibranairs
Spinners	Dominos
Starland Vocal Band	Danoffs
Statler Brothers	Kingsmen
Status Quo	Spectors/Traffic Jam
Steppenwolf	Sparrow
Stone the Crows	Power
Strawberry Alarm Clock	Sixpence
Styx	Tradewinds
Supremes	Primettes
Sweet	Sweetshop
Tavares	Chubby and the Turnpikes
Temptations	Primes
10 cc	Hot Legs
Three Dog Night	Redwood
Tower of Power	Motowns
Trens	Tremeloes
Turtles	Crossfires
Vanilla Fudge	Pigeons
Velvet Underground	Falling Spikes
Vogues	Val Aires
War	Night Shift
Watts 103rd Street Rhythm Band	Charles Wright & the Wright Sounds
Wet Willie	Fox
Who	High Numbers/Detours
Yardbirds	Metropolis Blues Quartet

Alan Price

Organist Alan Price left the up-and-coming British group the Animals because of his fear of flying.

Primrose Lane

In 1959 Jerry Wallace had rich success with a catchy song titled *Primrose Lane.* The song reappeared in 1970 as the theme song for the 1970 television series "The Smith Family," starring Henry Fonda.

Procol Harum

The group Procol Harum was named after Keith Reid's cat.

The Professors

The piano players (The Professors) of rock 'n' roll:

Hit Record	*Artist*	*Piano Player*
Rocket 88 (1951)	Jackie Brenston	Ike Turner
Lawdy Miss Clawdy (1952)	Lloyd Price	Fats Domino
Only You (1955)	Platters	Ernie Freeman
Canadian Sunset (1956)	Hugo Winterhalter	Eddie Heywood
Goodnight My Love (1956)	Jessie Belvin	Barry White
Heartbreak Hotel (1956)	Elvis Presley	Floyd Cramer
Matchbox (1956)	Carl Perkins	Jerry Lee Lewis
Jailhouse Rock (1957)	Elvis Presley	Mike Stoller

Hit Record	*Artist*	*Piano Player*
Sea Cruise (1959)	Frankie Ford	Huey "Piano" Smith
There Goes My Baby (1959)	Drifters	King Curtis
I'm Sorry (1960)	Brenda Lee	Floyd Cramer
Big Bad John (1961)	Jimmy Dean	Floyd Cramer
He's A Rebel (1962)	Crystals	Leon Russell
One Fine Day (1963)	Chiffons	Carole King
Little By Little (1964)	Rolling Stones	Gene Pitney
He Ain't Heavy, He's My Brother (1969)	Hollies	Elton John
Bridge Over Troubled Waters (1970)	Simon and Garfunkel	Larry Knechtel
You've Got A Friend(1971)	James Taylor	Carole King
Do You Want To Dance? (1972)	Bette Midler	Barry Manilow
To Know You Is To Love You (1973)	B. B. King	Stevie Wonder
Gentle On My Mind (1971)	Elvis Presley	Ronnie Milsap

Pseudonyms of Rock 'n' Roll Artists

Here are some pseudonyms and real names of rock 'n' roll artists:

Pseudonym	*Real Name*
Adam Faith	Terrence Nelhams
Alice Cooper	Vincent Furnier

Pseudonym	*Real Name*
Alvin Stardust	Bernard Jewry
Baby Huey	James Thomas Ramey
Ben E. King	Benjamin Nelson
Big Bopper	Jiles Perry Richardson
Billy J. Kramer	William Howard Ashton
Bo Diddley	Elias McDaniel
Bob Dylan	Robert Zimmerman
Bobby Darin	Robert Waldon Cassatto
Bobby Day	Robert Byrd
Bobby Rydell	Robert Louis Ridarelli
Bobby Vee	Robert Velline
Bonnie Tyler	Gaynor Hopkins
Brook Benton	Benjamin Franklin Peay
Buck Dharma	Donald Roeser
Buddy Holly	Charles Hardin Holley
Buzz Clifford	Reese Frances Clifford III
Captain Beefheart	Don Van Vliet
Carole King	Carole Klein
Cass Elliot	Naomi Cohen
Cat Stevens	Steven Georgiou
Chaka Kahn	Yvette Marie Stevens
Cher	Cheryl La Piere
Chubby Checker	Ernest Evans
Cliff Richard	Harry Robert Webb
Commander Cody	George Frayne
Connie Francis	Constance Franconero
Connie Stevens	Concetta Ann Ingolia
Conway Twitty	Harold Jenkins
Dale Hawkins	Delmar Allen
Dave "Baby" Cortez	David Clowney
David Bowie	David Jones
David Essex	David Cook
David Glitter	Paul Gadd

Pseudonym	*Real Name*
Dean Martin	Dino Crocetti
Del Shannon	Charles Westover
Denny Laine	Brian Hines
Dick Manitoba	Richard Blum
Dickey Doo	Gerry Granahan
Dinah Washington	Ruth Gordon
Dino Valenti	Chester Powers
Dobie Gray	Leonard Victor Ainsworth III
Dr. Hook	Ray Sawyer
Dr. John	Malcolm John Rebennack
Dodie Stevens	Geraldine Ann Pasquale
Donna Fargo	Yvonne Vaughn
Donovan	Donald P. Leitch
Dusty Springfield	Mary O'Brien
Eddie Money	Edward Mahoney
Elton John	Reginald Dwight
Elvis Costello	Declan Patrick McManus
Engelbert Humperdinck	Gerry Dorsey
Eric Clapton	Eric Clapp
Ernie K. Doe	Ernest Kador
Fee Waybill	John Waldo Waybill
Frankie Valli	Frank Castelluccio
Freddy Cannon	Fred Pocariello
Freddy Fender	Baldemar G. Huerta
Freddy King	Billy Myles
Freddie Mercury	Freddie Bulsara
Gary Glitter	Paul Gadd
Gene Chandler	Eugene Dixon
Gene Vincent	Vincent Eugene Craddock
Genya Raven	Goldie Zelkowitz
Guitar Slim	Eddie Jones

Pseudonym	*Real Name*
Guy Mitchell	Al Cernick
Howlin' Wolf	Chester Arthur Burnett
Iggy Pop	James Jewell Osterburg
Jack Scott	Jack Scafone, Jr.
Janis Ian	Janis Fink
Jesse Colin Young	Perry Miller
Jessi Colter	Miriam Johnson
Joey Dee	Joseph DiNicolo
John Denver	John Deutschendorf
Johnny Ace	John Marshall Alexander, Jr.
Johnny Rivers	John Ramistella
Johnny Rotten	Johnny Lydon
Joni James	Joan Carbello Babbo
Joni Mitchell	Roberta Joan Anderson
Junior Walker	Autry DeWalt, Jr.
Kiki Dee	Pauline Mathews
Len Barry	Leonard Borisoff
Lenny Kaye	Link Cromwell
Lightnin Slim	Otis Hicks
Linda Scott	Linda Joy Sampson
Little Milton	James Campbell
Little Stevie Wonder	Steveland Morris Hardaway
Lou Christie	Lugee Sacco
Lulu	Marie Laurie
Magic Dick	Richard Salwitz
Marc Bolan	Marc Feld
Maria Muldaur	Maria Grazia Ross Domenica D'Amato
Marky Ramone	Marc Bell
Marty Balin	Martin Buchwald

Pseudonym	*Real Name*
Meatloaf	Marvin Lee Aday
Mickey Most	Michael Peter Hayes
Mitch Ryder	Billy Levise
Muddy Waters	McKinley Morganfield
Nervous Norvus	Jimmy Drake
Nina Simone	Eunice Kathleen Waymon
Ozzy Osborne	John Osborne
Patti Labelle	Patricia Holt
Patti Page	Clara Ann Fowler
Peggy Lee	Norma Delores Egstrom
Peter Wolf	Peter Blankenfield
Phil Phillips	John Philip Baptiste
Phoebe Snow	Pheobe Laub
Reg Presley	Reg Ball
Richard T. Bear	Richie Gertstein
Rick Derringer	Rick Zehringer
Ritchie Valens	Richard Valenzuela
Rory Storm	Alan Caldwell
Sam the Sham	Domingo Samudio
Sandie Shaw	Sandra Goodrich
Sid Vicious	John Simon Richie
Skeeter Davis	Mary Francis Penick
Sly Stone	Sylvester Stewart
Smiley Lewis	Overton Lemon
Steven Tyler	Steven Tallarico
Taj Mahal	Henry Sainte Claire Fredericks-Williams
Tina Turner	Annie May Bullock
Tiny Tim	Herbert Khaury
Tom Jones	Thomas James Woodard
Tommy Ramone	Tommy Erdelyi
U.S. Bonds	Gary Anderson

Pseudonym	*Real Name*
Vikki Carr	Florencia Bisenta de Casillas Martinez Cardona
Wayne Fontana	Glyn Ellis
Willie DeVille	Willie Borsey

Q

Suzi Quatro

Singer Suzi Quatro played Leather Tuscadero on the television series "Happy Days."

Suzi's sister, Patti Quatro, is a member of the group Fanny.

Quicksilver

Two members of the group Quicksilver were born on September 4; two others were born on August 24.

R

Gerry Rafferty

Gerry Rafferty was one of the founders of Stealers Wheel.

Rain

In their 1966 song *Rain* the Beatles introduced the playing of tapes backwards. This innovation has since been utilized by the Beatles and other groups.

The Rainbows

In 1955 Don Convay, Billy Stewart, and Marvin Gaye, all sang with an obscure R&B group called the Rainbows. The group's biggest hit, *Mary Lee,* came that same year.

Raindrops Keep Falling On My Head

Burt Bacharach originally requested that Bob Dylan record his composition *Raindrops Keep Falling On My Head* for the 1969 movie *Butch Cassidy and the Sundance Kid*. B. J. Thomas was chosen after Dylan rejected the offer.

Ramblin' Gamblin' Man

Eagle member Glenn Frey was the rhythm guitar player on Bob Seger's first hit record in 1968, *Ramblin' Gamblin' Man.*

Ramblin' Man

The Allman Brothers' rocker *Ramblin' Man* can be heard in the background of a pub scene in the 1973 horror film *The Exorcist.*

Boots Randolph

Sax player Homer "Boots" Randolph holds the distinction of being the only musician to play on both a Buddy Holly recording and later an Elvis Presley release.

Rare Earth–Wayne Fontana

Both Rare Earth and British artist Wayne Fontana recorded for record labels that had the same name as they. Rare Earth recorded for Rare Earth Records while Wayne Fontana (and the Mindbenders) recorded on Fontana Records.

Raunchy

Bill Justis' 1957 instrumental composition *Raunchy* was originally titled *Backwoods.*

Raunchy was the instrumental which George Harrison played on his guitar for John Lennon when he was auditioning to be a member of the Quarrymen.

Lou Rawls

Listen closely to Sam Cooke's *Bring It On Home to Me* and one can hear Lou Rawls, uncredited, singing harmony with Cooke.

Lou Rawls was once an employee at the American Bandstand Studio in Philadelphia.

Record Labels Owned by Rock Artists and Composers

Label	*Founder*
All Platinum	Sylvia Robinson (of Mickey and Sylvia)
Apple Records	Beatles
B. T. Puppy Records	Tokens
Bamboo Records/ Mr. Chand Records	Gene Chandler
Boxcar Records	Elvis Presley
Brother Records	Beach Boys
Capricorn Records	Allman Brothers
Chisa Records	Hugh Masekela
Countryside Records	Michael Nesmith
Crazy Cajun Records	Freddy Fender
Curtom Records	Curtis Mayfield
Dark Horse Records	George Harrison
Fever Records	Otis Blackwell
Garpax Records	Gary Paxton
Grunt Records	Jefferson Airplane
Harvey Records	Harvey Fuqua
Improv Records	Tonny Bennett
Ivory Records	Ivory Joe Hunter
JAD Records	Johnny Nash
Joda Records	Johnny Nash
Joe Turner Records	Joe Turner and Dootsie Williams
Jotis Records	Otis Redding
Kolob Records	Osmonds

Label	*Founder*
Konk Records	Ray Davies
Little David Records	Flip Wilson
Manticore Records	Emerson, Lake & Palmer
Million Dollar Records	Harold Melvin
Neighborhood Records	Melanie
Palladium Records	Bob Seger
People Records	James Brown
Philles Records	Phil Spector
Racoon Records	Youngbloods
Reprise Records	Frank Sinatra
Ring' O Records	Ringo Starr
Rocket Records	Elton John
Rolling Stones Records	Rolling Stones
Sar Records	Sam Cooke
Shelter Records	Leon Russell
Soul Records	Johnny Rivers
Sounds of the South Records	Al Kooper
Straight Records/ Bizarre Records	Frank Zappa
Swan Song Records	Led Zeppelin
T-Neck Records	Isley Brothers
Tangerine Records	Ray Charles
Threshold Records	Moody Blues
Tri Phi Records	Harvey Fuqua
Turntable Records	Lloyd Price
UK Records	Jonathan King
U.S. Songs	Jerry Leiber, Mike Stoller, Burt Bacharach, Hal David.

Label	*Founder*
Unlimited Gold Records	Barry White
Veteran Records	Staff Sergeant Barry Sadler
Vibration Records	Sylvia Robinson (of Mickey and Sylvia)
Viv Records	Lee Hazelwood
Windsong Records	John Denver

Red Rubber Ball

Red Rubber Ball, the Cyrkle's only hit record, released in 1966, was written by Paul Simon and Bruce Woodley (of the Seekers).

Otis Redding

Soul singer Otis Redding was the manager of another soulful-sounding artist, Arthur Conley.

In 1967 Otis Redding replaced Elvis Presley as the top male vocalist in Britain.

Booker T. and the MGs were once the backup band for Otis Redding.

Jimmy Reed

Blues singer Jimmy Reed couldn't read, so at his recording sessions his wife would whisper the lyrics to him just seconds prior to his singing them. On some recordings his wife's soft voice can be heard.

Della Reese

In 1960 Della Reese became the first black artist to sing *The Star Spangled Banner* at the annual All Star Baseball Game.

Della Reese played the role of Della Rogers from 1976 to 1978 on the television series "Chico and the Man."

She was once a member of the Clara Ward Singers.

Martha Reeves

Martha Reeves, lead singer of Martha and the Vandellas, joined Detroit's Motown Records as a secretary after high school.

Regal Theatre

It was at the Detroit movie house, the Regal Theatre, where twelve-year-old Stevie Wonder recorded his first hit record live, *Fingertips,* in 1963.

Rejoice

Rejoice, by the Jefferson Airplane, was based on the James Joyce literary work *Ulysses.*

Renaldo and Clara

The four-hour movie *Renaldo and Clara* was written, directed and co-edited by Bob Dylan in 1978.

Paul Revere

Living up to his *real* name, Paul Revere was married on July 4, 1976, America's Bicentennial.

Paul Revere and the Raiders

Paul Revere and the Raiders was the first rock group to record for the Columbia Record label.

Revolver

The album cover for the Beatles' LP *Revolver* was designed by Klaus Voorman who was once a flute and bass player for Manfred Mann.

(Ghost) Riders in the Sky

In 1961 the Ramrods recorded their only successful release with (*Ghost*) *Riders in the Sky*. The song was written in 1949 by Stan Jones, a Hollywood actor who has appeared in such western films as *The Horse Soldiers* (1959), *Invitation to a Gunfighter* (1964), and *The Great Locomotive Chase* (1956). He even wrote the screenplay for the 1950 movie *Rio Grande* in which he also appeared.

The Rinky Dinks

In 1958 two versions of a top-ten song came out at the same time. Both Buddy Holly and a group called the Rinky Dinks released *Early In Morning*. The lead singer of the Rinky Dinks was Bobby Darin. The Rinky Dinks had previously recorded the very same song for Brunswick Records under the name the Ding Dongs. Buddy Holly thus recorded a song written by Bobby Darin.

The Rip Chords

Bruce Johnson and Terry Melcher (son of Doris Day) were the studio voices of the Rip-Chords, who hit the charts in 1963 with *Hey Little Cobra*.

Tex Ritter

Singing cowboy Tex Ritter, who sang the theme song of the 1952 movie *High Noon,* is the only person who is a member of both the Cowboy Hall of Fame and the Country Western Music Hall of Fame.

Marty Robbins

Country artist Marty Robbins totaled his Dodge stock car in the 1972 Daytona 500 when he hit a wall at 150 miles per hour.

Smokey Robinson

William "Smokey" Robinson, one-time lead singer of the Miracles, composed the hit songs *My Guy, Two Lovers,* and *You Beat Me To The Punch,* all of which Mary Wells charted.

Band, Kings of Rhythm

The first R&B record recorded by Bill Haley with the Saddlemen was a cover of *Rocket 88,* recorded on Essex Records in 1951.

Rocco and the Saints

Bobby Rydell and Frankie Avalon were both members of an obscure Philadelphia group named Rocco and the Saints. Rydell played drums while Avalon played trumpet.

Rock Around the Clock

Bill Haley and the Comets' classic *Rock Around the Clock* keeps cropping up in various movies. It was the theme of the 1955 movie *The Blackboard Jungle* (banned in Britain for eleven years). It was the original theme song on the television series "Happy Days." It was the first song played in the 1973 movie *American Graffiti,* and it was the song playing on the radio of a Chrysler convertible that Superman outruns in the 1978 movie *Superman.* Finally, back in 1956 a movie was even named for the song—*Rock Around the Clock.*

It became the first record to sell a million copies in Britain.

Rocket 88

Rocket 88 was one of the early R&B hits released in 1951 on Chess Records. It was performed by Jackie Brenston. The record was produced by Sam Phillips and the band backing Brenston was Ike Turner's.

Rockin' Robin

Rockin' Robin reached #2 in the Billboard charts for both Bobby Day (in 1958) and Michael Jackson (in 1972).

Jimmie Rodgers

On December 1, 1967, singer Jimmie Rodgers was mysteriously found in his car with a fractured skull. It was later discovered that he had been beaten up by an off-duty Los Angeles policeman. He has had to undergo several brain operations.

Rollin' Stone

It was Muddy Waters' (McKinley Morganfield) 1950 composition *Rollin' Stone* that would years later lend its name to a highly successful rock group and a highly successful rock newspaper.

The Ronettes

Sisters Veronica and Estelle Bennett, two-thirds of the Ronettes, were once employed as house dancers at the Peppermint Lounge.

Phil Spector recorded the Ronettes in a totally dark room so that Ronnie (Veronica) would not be distracted.

Linda Ronstadt

Linda Ronstadt sang at President Carter's Inauguration and for the opening game of the 1977 World Series, singing *The Star Spangled Banner* while wearing a Dodgers' baseball jacket.

The grandfather of superstar Linda Ronstadt was the inventor of the electric stove and the grease gun.

In April 1979 Linda Ronstadt and California governor Jerry Brown spent a week together in Africa.

Roosters

The obscure British group the Roosters produced three successful artists: Paul Jones, who became a member of Manfred Mann; Brian Jones who became a member of the Rolling Stones; and Eric Clapton.

Diana Ross

Diana Ross became the first entertainer ever to be invited to Japan's Imperial Palace. In 1973 Diana had an audience with Hirohito's wife, the empress of Japan.

Kendall Roundtree

Singer Little Willie John was sent to prison for manslaughter after the death of railroad employee Kendall Roundtree. It was while in prison at Washington State Penitentiary that John died of pneumonia on May 26, 1968.

Dick Rowe

In 1963 it was Dick Rowe, the executive with Decca Records, who turned down the Beatles, only to sign the Rolling Stones a few weeks later.

The Royal Teens

Al Kooper was once a member of the group the Royal Teens, who gave us *Short Shorts* in 1957. The composer of *Short Shorts,* Bob Gaudio, became a member of the Four Seasons, and Buddy Randell, another member, later joined the Knickerbockers.

RSO Records

In 1973 Robert Stigwood formed RSO Records (Robert Stigwood Organization). In April 1978, RSO Records had placed six singles in the Billboard top ten and their sound-track album *Saturday Night Fever* is now the biggest-selling album in history.

Ruby and the Romantics

The previous name of Ruby and the Romantics was the Supremes, a name that would become a classic for another female group.

Rumbo

In 1971 Dennis Wilson cut a single titled *Lady/ Sound of Free* with an artist named Rumbo credited on the record label. Rumbo was actually an assumed name used by Daryl "The Captain" Dragon.

Todd Rundgren

Todd Rundgren wrote, produced, arranged, sang, and played every instrument on his 1978 album *Hermit of Mink Hollow,* which produced the top 30 hit *Can We Still Be Friends* (#29).

Running Bear

Johnny Preston's biggest record was a novelty song titled *Running Bear* (1958). It was composed by J. P. Richardson, who became better known as the Big Bopper, whose voice can be heard in the background as one of the whooping Indians.

Bobby Russell

Composer Bobby Russell has been previously married to singer/comedian Vicki Lawrence.

Leon Russell

Leon Russell has been a mainstay in rock music. He has been a member of the Hawks; backed up Jerry

Lee Lewis, Conway Twitty, Anita Bryant, Patti Page, David Gates, Jimmy Webb, Merle Haggard; backed up Elvis Presley in his movies; been a Phil Spector sessions musician; produced Bob Dylan; played with the Rolling Stones; and was a member of Friends.

It was in the studio in Leon Russell's home where the Knickerbockers recorded *Lies* in 1965.

Leon Russell–David Gates

Leon Russell and David Gates were in the same Tulsa, Oklahoma, high school band together.

Russian Roulette

The haunting, strange game of Russian roulette has claimed two rock 'n' roll stars. In 1954 Johnny Ace and twenty-four years later in 1978 Terry Kath of the band Chicago lost their lives playing the deadly game.

Bobby Rydell

It was bandleader Paul Whiteman who gave Robert Lewis Ridarelli the popular stage name of Bobby Rydell.

In 1957 Bobby Rydell played drums in a Philadelphia band called Rocco and the Saints whose lead singer was Frankie Avalon.

Bobby Rydell played Hugo Peabody in the 1963 movie version of *Bye Bye Birdie.*

S

Barry Sadler

Green Beret member Staff Sergeant Barry Sadler had a number-one song in the United States in 1966. His record *The Ballad of the Green Berets* was one of the fastest records to move to first place that year.

Sergeant Barry Sadler posed for the cover of Robin Moore's novel *The Green Berets.*

In December of 1978 Barry Sadler shot and killed song writer Lee Emerson Bellamy.

Ed Sanders

Ed Sanders, the author of the biographical work about Charles Manson titled *The Family,* was once the lead singer of the Fugs.

Veronique Sanson

Veronique Sanson co-wrote (with Patti Dahlstrom) *Emotion* which Helen Reddy recorded in 1975. Veronique is the wife of Stephen Stills.

Mongo Santamaria

Mongo Santamaria, who in 1963 had a hit record titled *Watermelon Man,* was a musician on Ray Charles' 1957 release *Swanee River Rock.*

Saturday Night Fever

The album *Saturday Night Fever,* produced by the Bee Gees, is the greatest selling sound-track album of all time.

Save the Last Dance For Me

According to Paul McCartney, the Drifters' 1960 record *Save the Last Dance For Me* inspired him to compose *Hey Jude.*

Boz Scaggs

Boz Scaggs served as guitarist with the Steve Miller Band from 1967 through 1968.

Scrambled Eggs

The working title for the Paul McCartney–John Lennon ballad *Yesterday* was *Scrambled Eggs.*

Screamin' Jay Hawkins

Screamin' Jay Hawkins, whose bizarre act had him appearing out of a coffin with his skull prop Henry, was previously a Golden Glove Champion in 1947.

The Screw, (Do)

One of the rarest rock 'n' roll records is the 1963 Crystals' version of *(Do) The Screw,* Part I and II. I doubt if it ever received any A.M. air time.

Sea Cruise

When Frankie Ford recorded the rock classic *Sea Cruise* with Huey "Piano" Smith's band, he actually sang over the vocal of Smith on the tape, leaving the original recording intact except for his voice.

Jim Seals

Jim Seals of Seals and Crofts was at one time the Texas State Fiddle Champion.

Seals and Crofts

Seals and Crofts perform the theme song *The First Years* for the television series "Paper Chase."

John Sebastian

It was in John Sebastian's home where the group Crosby, Stills and Nash was formed, evolving from a jam session into a highly respected group.

Secret Agent Man

The theme song *Secret Agent Man* from the British television series "Secret Agent," starring Patrick McGoohan, was sung by Johnny Rivers.

Neil Sedaka

Arthur Rubinstein selected Neil Sedaka as the best classical pianist in New York City in 1956.

Neil Sedaka dedicated his song *The Immigrant* to John Lennon who at the time was fighting deportation from the United States. (He wasn't deported.)

In his youth, Neil Sedaka once wrote a song a day for one year.

Neil Sedaka and his co-writer Howard Greenfield wrote the score for the 1960 movie *Where the Boys Are* in which Connie Francis made her debut.

Bob Seger

While a track man in high school, Bob Seger once ran a 5:05-minute mile.

Seventh Sons

Glen Campbell, Eddie Dean, and Perry Como are all said to be the seventh son of a seventh son. According to Robert L. Ripley, Russ Columbo, the popular crooner of the 1940s was the twelfth son of a twelfth son.

Sha Na Na

Sha Na Na borrowed their name from the lyrics of the Silhouettes' 1957 hit song *Get a Job*.

Sandie Shaw

British singer Sandie Shaw had the unique gimmick of always singing barefooted. The group Procol

Harum was originally Shaw's backup band when they were known as the Paramounts.

The Shadows

The British group the Shadows played a dual role, as the leading instrumental group of England and as the backup band on most of Cliff Richard's hit records. They originally called themselves the Drifters until it was discovered that there already existed an American group by that name.

Del Shannon

Del Shannon was the first American to cover a Beatles song when in 1963 he recorded *From Me To You* on Big Top Records.

Sh-Boom

The Chords' 1954 version of *Sh-Boom* is considered by many to have been the first vocal rock 'n' roll record.

James Shepperd

In 1956 James Shepperd sang lead on the Heartbeats' ballad *A Thousand Miles Away.* In 1961 another group called Shep and the Limelites recorded an answer record titled *Daddy's Home.* It was James Shepperd again who sang lead.

Shimmy Shimmy Ko-Ko-Bop

It was during the playing of Little Anthony and the Imperials' *Shimmy Shimmy Ko-Ko-Bop* that Alan

Freed sadly told his listening audience in November 1959 on radio station WABC in New York that he had been fired.

Shindig

Some of the members of the orchestra on the 1960 television series "Shindig" were piano player Leon Russell, guitarists Glen Campbell, David Gates, and organist Billy Preston.

Jimmy O'Neill, host of the series, was married to composer Sharon Sheeley.

The Shirelles

The Gospelaires were a gospel group that recorded several demo records for the Shirelles. The lead singer of the group was Dionne Warwick.

Short People

Randy Newman's controversial novelty song *Short People* was banned on a number of radio stations.

Shutters and Boards

In 1962 Jerry Wallace had a minor hit with the country song *Shutters and Boards.* The song was composed by Scott Turner and World War II hero Audie Murphy.

Signed, Sealed and Delivered

One of the co-writers on Stevie Wonder's hit *Signed, Sealed and Delivered* was his mother Lulu Hardaway.

Enrique Antonio Silvestor

Enrique Antonio Silvestor of the Main Ingredient is the grandson of the first president of the country of Panama.

Carly Simon

Singer Carly Simon is the daughter of Richard Simon, the co-founder of the large publishing house of Simon and Schuster. Among the many visitors to her house when Carly was a child was Albert Einstein.

Carly Simon is the wife of singer James Taylor.

Paul Simon

Paul Simon played the bit role of record producer in the 1977 Academy Award winning movie *Annie Hall.*

Paul Simon once taught at New York University, one of his students being Melissa Manchester.

Nancy Sinatra

Nancy Sinatra is probably the only singer who had a song written about her when she was born. Jimmy Van Heusen and Phil Silvers composed *Nancy with the Laughin' Face* for her. Her father Frank Sinatra later recorded the song.

Singing the Blues

In case you've wondered who is whistling on Guy Mitchell's 1956 hit record *Singing the Blues,* it wasn't Guy, but orchestra leader Ray Conniff.

Skip and Flip

Skip Battin, who was once a member of the 1960s duet Skip and Flip, became a member of the Byrds, replacing John York.

Slade

The group Slade often intentionally misspelled the titles of their songs. The original name of the group was Ambrose Slade until shortened by their manager Chas Chandler.

Slippin' and Slidin'

Little Richard's 1956 R & B classic *Slippin' and Slidin'* was originally recorded under the title of *I Got the Blues for You* by Al Collins (the very first record released on the Ace label). The lyrics were then changed by Eddie Bo and the song became *I'm Wise*. Finally it was changed to *Slippin' and Slidin'* which has been recorded by Little Richard, Buddy Holly, and others.

Smile

In 1954, Nat "King" Cole had a hit on Capitol Records with the ballad *Smile*. *Smile* had been composed that year by Geoffrey Parsons, John Turner, and actor Charlie Chaplin.

Connie Smith

Country singer Connie Smith was once a member of Eddie Cochran's backup band the Kelly 4.

Huey "Piano" Smith and the Clowns

The New Orleans group Huey "Piano" Smith and the Clowns had two classic hits in 1957 and 1958, titled *Rocking Pneumonia and the Boogie Woogie Flu* and *Don't You Just Know It.* The lead singer of the group was Bobby Marchan, who in 1960 had a hit with *There's Something On Your Mind.* The sax player was Lee Allen who played on sessions with Fats Domino and Little Richard and in 1958 had a hit with *Walkin' With Mr. Lee.* The trumpet player was Alvin "Red" Tyler who had an instrumental hit in 1961 titled *Snake Eyes.* And of course Huey Smith was the band's piano player who also wrote the 1958 Frankie Ford hit song *Sea Cruise.* The group also backed up Jimmy Clanton on his 1958 record *Just A Dream.*

O. C. Smith

O. C. Smith was once a vocalist with Count Basie's Orchestra.

Hank Snow

Singer Hank Snow is the only prominent country artist to be born in Liverpool. That is, of course, Liverpool, Nova Scotia.

So Rare

As Jimmy Dorsey passed away in a New York hospital in March 1957, his single *So Rare* made the top ten of the rock 'n' roll-oriented hit parade. His band would have their last chart hit later that year with a two-sided smash, *Jay Dee's Boogie Woogie* backed by *June Night*.

In 1958 Tommy Dorsey's orchestra would be the last big band to make the charts with *Tea for Two Cha Cha*, although Tommy himself had died in 1956.

Sonny and Cher

When Sonny and Cher were first singing together as a duet, they sang under the name of Caesar and Cleo.

Soupy Sales

Comedian Soupy Sales' sons Tony (guitarist) and Hunt (drummer) are notable session musicians who've played with such artists as David Bowie and Iggy Pop.

Joe South

Joe South was one of the session musicians on Bob Dylan's 1966 album *Blonde On Blonde*.

South Philadelphia

South Philadelphia is the birthplace of the following singers: Mario Lanza, Eddie Fisher, Bobby Rydell, Frankie Avalon, Al Martino, Fabian Forte, Charlie Gracie, Chubby Checker, Jim Croce, James Darren, and Buddy Greco. Many of them attended the same high school—South Philadelphia High.

Southern Nights

The photograph for Glen Campbell's *Southern Nights* album cover was taken by Kenny Rogers.

Spanish Harlem

Ben E. King's *Spanish Harlem* was composed by the combined talents of Jerry Leiber and Phil Spector, their only joint composition.

Specialty Records

The Los Angeles based record label Specialty Records had a formula for hit records with catchy titles sung by talented artists in the 1950s such as:

Lawdy Miss Clawdy (1952)	Lloyd Price
Long Tall Sally (1956)	Little Richard
Short Fat Fanny (1957)	Larry Williams
Bony Moronie (1957)	Larry Williams
Dizzy Miss Lizzy (1958)	Larry Williams
Good Golly Miss Molly (1958)	Little Richard

On the flip side of *Bony Moronie* was the hit *You Bug Me Baby,* composed by Sonny Bono.

Phil Spector

Teenage millionaire record producer Phil Spector married, but later divorced, Ronnie Bennett, the lead singer of one of his groups, the Ronnettes.

Spector never recorded his record sessions in stereo. He played a small role in the 1969 Dennis Hopper movie *Easy Rider*.

One of the musicians on the Rolling Stones' hit *Play With Fire* was Phil Spector, playing guitar.

He was one of the background singers on George Harrison's *My Sweet Lord.*

Spirit

Ed Cassidy, the drummer for Spirit, is the stepfather of lead guitarist Randy California.

Dusty Springfield

Soulful British singer Dusty Springfield sang the original theme song for the television series "The Six Million Dollar Man," though the song was later dropped.

Bruce Springsteen

Singer Bruce Springsteen appeared simultaneouly on the cover of *Time* and *Newsweek,* the week of October 27, 1975.

Springsteen enjoyed royalties for three successive years as the writer/co-writer of three different hits for three different artists: 1977 (#1) *Blinded by the Light*—Manfred Mann's Earthband; 1978 (#13) *Because the Night*—Patti Smith (co-written); 1979 (#2) *Fire*—Pointer Sisters.

Stagger Lee

When ABC Paramount released Lloyd Price's huge hit record *Stagger Lee* in 1959, they were met with protests because the lyrics mentioned a man gambling over a woman. The record was reissued with new lyrics about a man gambling for a Stetson hat. The song still went to number one.

The Starland Vocal Band

Under the group's original name of Fat City, the Starland Vocal Band provided the vocal background for John Denver's 1971 hit *Take Me Home, Country Roads.*

On the strength of only one hit record—*Afternoon Delight* in 1979—the group hosted their own TV series in 1977 called "The Starland Vocal Band."

Ringo Starr–Billy Fury

Richard Starkey, better known as Ringo Starr, attended the Dingle Vale Secondary Modern School at the same time as another British rock artist Ronald Wycherley, better known as Billy Fury.

Ringo Starr–Stephen Stills–Peter Sellers

Ringo Starr, Stephen Stills, and Peter Sellers have all been the owners of the same house in Surrey, England.

Steam Packet

The British group Steam Packet was gifted with such members as John Baldry, Brian Auger, Julie Driscoll, Rod Stewart, and Elton John.

Steely Dan

Group members Donald Fagen and Walter Becker of Steely Dan were both previously members of Jay and the Americans.

Frank N. Stein

Whenever Elton John signs a hotel register, he signs the name Frank N. Stein. (Marlon Brando registers as Lord Greystoke.)

Jim Steinman

Pianist Jim Steinman of Meat Loaf lived in the same fraternity house at Amherst College as did David Eisenhower.

Steppenwolf

Steppenwolf, the group that took its name from a Hermann Hesse novel, was previously called Sparrow.

Dodie Stevens

Dodie Stevens (born Geraldine Ann Pasquale) had one hit record *Pink Shoe Laces* and appeared in one hit movie *Hound Dog Man,* both in the same year, 1959. In the 1960s Dodie Stevens became a singer with Sergio Mendez and Brazil '66. Still later, she became a back-up singer for Mac Davis.

Ray Stevens

Singer Ray Stevens of *Ahab the Arab* fame was a hand clapper on the Archies' 1969 number-one hit *Sugar, Sugar.*

The Steve Miller Band

When Chuck Berry recorded his album *Live at the Fillmore* in 1967, the group that backed him was the Steve Miller Band.

On the Steve Miller *Anthology* album, Paul McCartney played bass and drums for some of the cuts.

•

John Stewart

John Stewart, one of the members of the Kingston Trio (he replaced Dave Guard) composed the Monkees' 1968 hit *Daydream Believer.*

Rod Stewart–Raymond Davies

Rod Stewart and Raymond Davies of the Kinks both played football for the same school team in England.

Sticky Fingers

Artist Andy Warhol designed the album cover for the Rolling Stones LP, *Sticky Fingers.*

Steve Stills

It was artist Steve Stills who recommended Peter Tork to become one of the four Monkees.

Mike Stoller

Producer and composer Mike Stoller (half of the phenomenal team of Mike Stoller and Jerry Leiber) is the piano player on Elvis Presley's 1957 hit *Jailhouse Rock.*

Sly Stone

During the intermission of a performance at Madison Square Garden in 1974, Sly Stone married Kathy Silva on stage.

At age 19 Sly Stone produced the San Francisco hits *Laugh Laugh* and *Just a Little* for the Beau Brummels. He also produced (with Grace Slick) the Great Society's biggest record, *Somebody To Love.*

Bobby Freeman's 1964 hit *C'mon and Swim* was composed and produced by Sly Stone.

Sylvester "Sly" Stone and major league pitcher Tug McGraw were school mates at Vallejo Junior High in Vallejo, California.

Stormy

The Classic IV's 1969 hit *Stormy* was penned by J. R. Cobb, a member of the Atlanta Rhythm Section.

Stormy Weather

The rarest R & B record and also the most valuable is the Five Sharps' 1952 version of *Stormy Weather* on Jubilee Records. Not even Jubilee Records owns a copy. The 78 RPM is valued at over $4000.

Story Untold

When the Nutmegs originally recorded their oldie ballad *Story Untold,* the song was titled *Deep In My Heart There's A Story Untold,* the song running for over three minutes. But it was difficult in the 1950s to get a record played on the air that ran for over three minutes, so the group rerecorded the song, reducing its length to 2:20 and also reducing the title to *Story Untold.*

Stranger On the Shore

When ATCO Records released the instrumental *Stranger on the Shore* in 1962, the British artist was credited on the label as *Mr.* Acker Bilk. The record went to the number-one position in both England and the United States.

Jenny was the original title of *Stranger on the Shore.*

Street Fighting Man

During the infamous Democratic Convention held in Chicago in 1968, the Rolling Stones hit *Street Fighting Man* was actually banned on Chicago radio stations.

Barbra Streisand

Barbra Streisand was nominated for a Tony for her first Broadway play, *I Can Get It for You Wholesale.* She won an Oscar for her first movie *Funny Girl*

(1967), a Grammy for her first record album *The Barbra Streisand Album* (1963), and an Emmy for her first television special "Color Me Barbra" (1965). She has twice been elected to the International Best Dressed List and in 1977 won another Oscar with Paul Williams for the song *Evergreen.*

Barbra Streisand and Neil Diamond both sang in the same school choir with one another at New York City's Eramus Hall High School. In 1978 the pair recorded *You Don't Bring Me Flowers.*

Stylistics

The Philadelphia group the Stylistics was formed when the two groups the Monarchs and the Percussions joined forces.

Sugarloaf

All five members of Sugarloaf, outside of lead singer Jerry Corbetta, are named Bob.

Sukiyaki

The only Japanese hit song to reach number one in the United States was *Sukiyaki* by Kyu Sakamoto, released in 1963.

Barry Sullivan

Actor Barry Sullivan is the father-in-law of musician Jim Messina.

Summertime

On the flip side of Sam Cooke's *You Send Me,* released on the Keene Record label in 1957 (his first hit record which went all the way to number one), is an excellent rendition of *Summertime* with a slight calypso beat. When RCA Victor began releasing Sam Cooke's music on their label, *Summertime* then became a slow ballad rather than the excellent original version. In many cases RCA Victor will list the ballad as *Summertime Part 2,* although they have never released Part 1.

Summertime and Fever

The very first record by the Beatles was made in late 1960 at the Akustik Studio in Hamburg, Germany. The Beatles backed up a singer from another Liverpool group, Rory Storm and the Hurricanes, named Wally. They recorded the two songs *Summertime* and *Fever* on one side of the 78 RPM acetate (the other side was a radio advertisement for leather goods). Ironically, John, Paul, and George asked to use the Hurricanes' drummer Ringo Starr on the recording instead of their own drummer Pete Best.

Sun Records

Memphis recording company Sun Records, located at 706 Union Avenue, was founded by Sam Phillips in 1951. Between 1954 and 1957 these stars recorded under the Sun label: Elvis Presley, Johnny Cash, Jerry Lee Lewis, Carl Perkins, Harold Dorman, David Huston, Roy Orbison, Charlie Rich and Conway Twitty (under his real name Harold Jenkins). Ike Turner was once a talent scout for the label. The Johnny Burnett Trio also cut some tapes for Sun but they were never released. Soul artist B. B. King and Junior Parker also recorded for Sun Records in the early 1950s.

The Sunliners

When the white group the Sunliners began to record for the Motown label, the name of the group was changed and a new label was formed, both named Rare Earth.

The Supremes

When Diana Ross left the Supremes for a solo career, Jean Terrell replaced her as lead singer of the Supremes. Jean was the sister of heavyweight boxer Ernie Terrell.

The Supremes have had ten number-one hit songs in the Billboard charts (five of them were consecutive).

The Supremes recorded one 45 RPM under their original name the Primettes. Titled *Tears of Sorrow/ Pretty Baby* it was released on the Lupine Record label and is today a collectors item.

The Supremes are the most popular female vocal group of all time.

Superstar

The Carpenters' 1971 release *Superstar* was written by Leon Russell and Bonnie Bramlett.

Supertramp

Roger Hodgson of the band Supertramp helped to deliver his wife Karuna's baby girl Heidi Hodgson, with only twelve minutes left to stage time at a San Diego concert.

Surf City

Surf City was a number-one record for Jan and Dean in 1963. The song was originally composed by Brian Wilson, who can be heard singing on the record.

Surfin' U.S.A.

The Beach Boys' 1963 hit *Surfin' U.S.A.* borrowed the tune from Chuck Berry's 1958 classic *Sweet Little Sixteen,* with Brian Wilson rewriting the lyrics. When the Beach Boys version was released, only Brian Wilson was credited as composer. After litigation in which the song was rightfully credited to Chuck Berry, Chuck Berry is now shown as the only composer of *Surfin U.S.A.*

Surrealistic Pillow

Jerry Garcia of the Grateful Dead played guitar on the Jefferson Airplane's *Surrealistic Pillow.*

Survivors

In 1963 a group called the Survivors released a song titled *Pamela Jean* which sounded identical to the Beach Boys hit *Car Crazy Cutie.* There was no plagiarism suit since the Survivors were actually the Beach Boys.

Suzy and the Red Stripes

In 1977 an obscure group called Suzy and the Red Stripes recorded a record titled *Seaside Woman.* It was later discovered to actually be Linda McCartney performing on the record.

Billy Swan

Billy Swan once served as chauffeur to country singer Webb Pierce, driving Pierce's gaudy Silver Dollar automobile.

Billy Swan's voice can be heard saying "four" at the lead on Tony Joe White's version of *Polk Salad Annie.*

It was Billy Swan who composed the Clyde McPhatter hit *Lover Please.*

Billy Swan–Kris Kristofferson

Both Billy Swan and Kris Kristofferson were once employed as janitors at Nashville's Columbia Records Studio.

Billy Swan and Zal Yanovsky (lead guitarist of the Lovin' Spoonful) were both members of the Band of Thieves, Kris Kristofferson's band.

Sweet Inspirations

The three-girl group the Sweet Inspirations were the backup vocalists for Elvis Presley. The trio originally was formed to backup Aretha Franklin. Aretha's sister Carolyn led the group.

Sweet Little Angel

It was Ike Turner who composed B.B. King's classic hit *Sweet Little Angel.*

Sweet Soul Music

Stax artist Arthur Conley's *Sweet Soul Music* was written and first recorded by Sam Cooke as *Yeah Man.*

Switched On Bach

Walter Carlos, who recorded the best-selling moog album *Switched On Bach,* underwent a sex-change operation and is today known as Wendy Carlos.

Sylvester

Soul/disco artist Sylvester is a distant relative (cousin once removed) to the late blues singer "Lady Day," Billie Holiday.

T

Take A Message To Mary

In the 1957 Everly Brothers hit *Take A Message to Mary,* the sharp tinking sound heard is a screwdriver hitting a coke bottle.

Talking Heads

The New York rock group Talking Heads has quite an impressive academic background. Drummer Chriss Frantz is the son of a general, his wife is bassist Tina Weymouth, and along with singer/songwriter/guitarist David Byrne, all graduated from the exclusive Rhode Island School of Design. And to make things more interesting, keyboard/guitarist Jerry Harrison is a graduate of Harvard.

Tall Cool One

The Wailers' first record *Tall Cool One,* released in 1961 on the Golden Crest label, has the distinction of being the first hit rock 'n' roll record to show a picture of the group on the record label.

Tall Paul

Annette's 1959 hit *Tall Paul,* recorded on Disney's Buena Vista label, was previously recorded by another Mousketeer, Judy Harriet, but it was Annette's version that made the charts.

Tallahassee Lassie

In 1959 *Tallahassee Lassie* became the first hit song for Freddy Cannon. The song's composer was Freddy's mother, Mrs. Annette Picariello.

Tamla

William "Smokey" Robinson named his daughter Tamla after his friend Berry Gordy, Jr.'s first record label, Tamla Records of Detroit.

Tapestry

Both Don MacLean and Carole King have recorded albums titled *Tapestry*. Although MacLean's was not a success, King's became the all-time best-selling album up to that date.

The Tarriers

In 1956 an obscure calypso group called the Tarriers emerged with two hits, *The Banana Boat Song* and *Cindy, Oh Cindy*. Members of this aggregation were future actor Alan Arkin and Erik Darling, who in 1963 would form the Rooftop Singers.

Bernie Taupin

Songwriter Bernie Taupin met his co-writer Elton John when both men answered the same newspaper ad by Liberty Records advertising for songwriters.

Chip Taylor

Singer/composer Chip Taylor is the brother of Oscar-winning actor Jon Voight.

James Taylor and Carly Simon

Husband and wife James Taylor and Carly Simon served as best man and maid of honor at the August 23, 1978 marriage of Kate Jackson to Andrew Stevens.

Johnnie Taylor

Johnnie Taylor replaced Sam Cooke as the lead singer of the gospel group the Soul Stirrers.

Johnnie Taylor, who had a million-selling hit with *Disco Lady*, is an ordained minister.

Ted Taylor

Lancashire butcher Ted Taylor was the man who recorded the Beatles live at the Star Club in Hamburg Germany in 1962. Taylor was a member of the rock group the Dominoes whom he set up the tape recorder to record. The tapes were at first lost for a number of years but were found and worked on at a studio. They were released in the 1977 album *The Beatles Live! at the Star-Club in Hamburg, Germany, 1962.*

Taylors

James Taylor, his brother Livingston and their sister Kate have all spent time in a medical institution suffering from nerves (McLean Psychiatric Hospital). Their father, Dr. Isaac Taylor, is the Dean of the University of North Carolina Medical School.

Teen Angel

Mark Dinning's 1959 chart-buster *Teen Angel* was banned from British radio as too morbid.

Teen Commandments

In 1958 a trio of ABC Paramount artists recorded a song that I'm sure they'd like to forget today. Paul Anka, George Hamilton IV, and Johnny Nash recorded a do-and-don't lecture for fans titled *The Teen Commandments.*

Teen Kings

When Roy Orbison first recorded *Ooby Dooby* on Jew-el records in 1955, the label credited the song to the Teen Kings. On moving to Sun label, Orbison was then credited on the label of the Sun release of *Ooby Dooby.*

Teenage Idol

Teenage Idol (1962) was the last song in which Rick Nelson was credited on the record label as Ricky Nelson. Thereafter he was credited as Rick Nelson.

Teenage Lament '74

On Alice Cooper's recording of *Teenage Lament '74,* Liza Minnelli, Ronnie Spector, and Norma and Sarah LaBelle sang backup vocal.

Television Cartoon Series

The Beatles, the Monkees and Bay City Rollers have each had television cartoon series made about them. Ironically the group the Archies, who in 1969 had the number-one song of the year with *Sugar Sugar, was* a television cartoon group.

Television Song Debuts

The following three songs actually were premiered on television plays prior to each becoming hit records: *Teenage Crush* by Tommy Sands debuted on the Kraft Television Theatre's presentation of "The Singing Idol," broadcast in January 1957; *Start Movin'* by Sal Mineo debuted on the Kraft Television Theatre's presentation of "Drummer Man," broadcast in May of 1957; *Let Me Go Lover* by Joan Weber debuted on Studio One's presentation of "Let Me Go Lover," broadcast on November 15, 1954.

Television Theme Songs

Below is a list of TV series, with the artist who performed the theme song for each:

Series	*Artist*
"Maude"	Donny Hathaway
"Mary Tyler Moore Show"	Sonny Curtis
"Ironside"	Quincy Jones
"Chico and the Man"	José Feliciano
"Baretta"	Sammy Davis Jr.
"Courtship of Eddie's Father"	Nilsson
"The Rebel"	Johnny Cash
"Movin' On"	Merle Haggard
"Secret Agent"	Johnny Rivers
"Zorro"	Chordettes
"Welcome Back, Kotter"	John Sebastian
"Beverly Hillbillies"	Lester Flatt and Earl Scruggs
"The Associates"	B. B. King

Nino Tempo

In the 1954 biographical movie *The Glenn Miller Story,* Nino Tempo played the role of Wilbur Schwartz.

Temptations—Supremes

Prior to their success on Motown Records, the Temptations were known as the Primes. At a Detroit High School a female group named themselves the Primettes after the Primes whom they admired. This group would one day become the most famous female group of all time—the Supremes.

10 cc

10 cc was originally called Hot Legs. It was 10 cc who backed up Neil Sedaka on his hit songs in the 1970s.

Eric Stewart, a member of 10 cc, sang lead on *A Groovy Kind of Love* (1966) by the Mindbenders.

Ten Commandments of Love

If you listen carefully to the lyrics of Harvey and the Moonglows' 1958 ballad the *Ten Commandments of Love,* you'll hear someone blow their lines.

Texas Towns

Here are only a few of the Texas towns that inspired popular country songs:

Houston—Dean Martin
Abilene—George Hamilton IV
El Paso—Marty Robbins
San Antonio—Bob Wills (San Antonio Rose)
Amarillo—Neil Sedaka
Galveston—Glen Campbell
Laredo—Marty Robbins (The Streets of Laredo)
Lubenbach, Texas—Waylon Jennings

That'll Be the Day

Buddy Holly and the Crickets' 1957 hit *That'll Be the Day* was inspired by one of John Wayne's lines in the 1956 movie *The Searchers.* The song *That'll Be the Day* would, in 1973, inspire a rock movie by that same name. The British group the Searchers took their name from the same John Wayne film.

When *That'll Be the Day* was first released in 1957, it was on the Decca Record label and credited to Buddy Holly and the Three Tunes.

When noted record producer Owen Bradley first heard *That'll Be the Day* by the Crickets, he said that it was the worst song he'd ever heard.

That'll Be the Day was the first tune which John Lennon learned to play on his first guitar.

There Goes My Baby

There Goes My Baby, a 1959 top-ten record by the Drifters, holds the distinction as being the first rhythm-and-blues record to utilize violins.

There Is No Such Person in the Band

The following groups were named after a person who is not a member of the group:

Babe Ruth
Barefoot Jerry
Charlie
Crabby Appleton
Derek and the Dominos
Dr. Feelgood
Dr. Hook
Henry Cow
Jethro Tull
Jo Jo Gunne
Kilburn and the High Roads
King Crimson
Lynyrd Skynyrd
Marshal Tucker Band

Max Demian Band
Moby Grape
Molly Hatchet
Mott (The Hoople)
Pablo Cruise
Rufus
Savoy Brown
(Ambrose) Slade
Steely Dan
T. Rex
Toby Beau
Uriah Heep
Vinegar Joe
Wet Willie

There's A Moon Out Tonight

The Capris' 1960 hit *There's A Moon Out Tonight* was released on four different labels in 1960: Planet Records, Lost Nite Records, Old Town Records, and Trommers Records.

The Thing

Little Richard (Penniman) originally titled his biggest hit *Long Tall Sally, The Thing.*

Carla Thomas

Carla Thomas, whose biggest hit was *Gee Whiz,* is the daughter of soul singer Rufus Thomas, whose biggest hit was *Walkin' the Dog*. The duet of Carla Thomas and Otis Redding had a top-ten hit in 1967 with *Tramp.*

Those Were the Days

Mary Hopkin made popular *Those Were the Days* in 1968 on Apple Records. The song is actually based on the Russian folk song *Darogoi Dimmoyo*.

Three Dog Night

Three Dog Night was named after the Australian Aborigines' custom of sleeping with three dogs on an extremely cold night. The term was found in a copy of *Mankind Magazine*.

Danny Hutton of Three Dog Night once did the voices for Hanna-Barbera television cartoon characters.

The Three Flames

The Three Flames was one of a number of groups to record a version of *Open The Door Richard* between 1946 and 1947. However in 1949, the trio hosted their own national network TV series called the "The Three Flames Show," shown on NBC from June 13 to August 20, 1949.

Three Steps to Heaven

Three Steps to Heaven was a song by Eddie Cochran released at the time of his death in 1960.

Thunder Road

The Ballad of Thunder Road was written and recorded by actor Robert Mitchum for the 1958 movie

Thunder Road. Elvis Presley was offered but turned down the lead role, which Mitchum then played.

Tico and the Triumphs

In 1962 Tico and the Triumphs had a minor hit with *Motorcycle*. The lead guitarist on the record was Paul Simon.

Time Magazine

The following artists have had their individual pictures on the cover of Time: Harry Belafonte (1959); Joan Baez (1962); the Beatles (1967); Aretha Franklin (1968); the Band (1970); James Taylor (1971); Joni Mitchell (1974); Bruce Springsteen (1975); Cher (1975); Elton John (1975); Paul McCartney (1976); Linda Rondstadt (1977).

To Know Him Is To Love Him

In 1958 a smooth ballad by the Teddy Bears titled *To Know Him Is To Love Him* climbed the charts to the top. One of the members of the trio was named Phil Spector who composed the song when he was inspired by the inscription on his father's tombstone. The drummer on the record was Sandy Nelson.

Nick Todd

In 1957 an obscure artist named Nick Todd had a one-hit record titled *Plaything*. Nick Todd is Pat Boone's brother. The name Todd came from reversing the word Dot, the record label on which both brothers recorded.

The Tokens

The Tokens, whose biggest hit was *The Lion Sleeps Tonight,* was originally the group with whom Neil Sedaka sang at Abraham Lincoln High in Brooklyn.

Tom & Jerry

The 1950s rock 'n' roll duet Tom (Graph) and Jerry (Landis) was the name originally used by Paul Simon and Art Garfunkel. *Hey Schoolgirl* on Big Records in 1957 was their only hit.

Tomorrow Night

In 1955 while recording for Sun Records, Elvis Presley cut a number of songs which RCA Victor bought the rights to when they purchased Elvis' contract from Sun owner Sam Phillips. One of these songs was titled *Tomorrow Night,* and was finally released ten years later in 1965 with the addition of the Anita Kerr Singers singing background vocal.

Tornadoes

The first British group to have an American number-one hit was the Tornadoes in 1962 with *Telstar*. The group was formed when the members answered an advertisement in a London paper. The members then met one another for the first time.

Tower of Power

In 1976 Rick Stevens, the lead singer of Tower of Power, was found guilty of first degree murder of three men.

The horn section of the group Tower of Power can be heard on Elton John's *Caribou* album.

Town Without Pity

Prior to Gene Pitney's recording *Town Without Pity*, the theme from the United Artists movie of that name, the song was offered by Don Costa to Vito Picone, the lead singer of the Elegants. Because of his loyalty to his vocal group, Picone turned down the solo opportunity. His group never had another hit record.

Tragedy

In 1959 the obscure Fernwood record label released *Tragedy* by Thomas Wayne. The song became a rock 'n' roll classic. A few years later the record was reissued with violins added in the background. The original version, as in most cases, is the better.

Transfusion

In 1956 a novelty record titled *Transfusion* was recorded by the Four Jokers. One of the group's members, James Drake, recorded the same song under the pseudonym of Nervous Norvus and had the hit version.

Travelin' Man

The 1958 Ricky Nelson hit *Travelin' Man* was composed by Jerry Fuller (originally for Sam Cooke). Jerry Fuller, Glen Campbell, and Dave Burgess sang on the demo.

Jay Traynor

Jay Traynor, the lead singer of Jay and the Americans, was previously a member of the late 1950s group the Mystics, whose biggest hit was *Hushabye.*

Tribute Records

Here's a list of singers who have had songs written in tribute to them:

Eddie Cochran—*Just Like Eddie* by Heinz
Patsy Cline—*Sing it for Us Patsy* by Freddie Hart
Buddy Holly—*American Pie* by Don MacLean
Ritchie Valens, Big Bopper, Buddy Holly—*Three Stars* by Tommy Dee
Johnny Ace—*Salute to Johnny Ace* by Ravens
Jimi Hendrix—*Song for a Dreamer* by Procol Harum

Troubadour

The Los Angeles nightclub the Troubadour is where Elton John made his U.S. debut on August 25, 1970.

John Lennon was thrown out of the Troubadour when he began heckling the Smother Brothers during their performances in March 1978.

The last group to play at the famed Troubadour was Orleans.

On May 15, 1973 the Pointer Sisters made their debut at the Troubadour on Santa Monica Boulevard.

Bobby Troup

Composer and husband of Julie London (Troup and London appear together on the television series "Emergency"), Bobby Troup is the composer of songs recorded by Little Richard (*The Girl Can't Help It*) and by the Rolling Stones (*Route 66*).

Doris Troy

In 1970 Doris Troy cut an album for Apple records titled *Doris Troy.* On the session of that album were: Billy Preston, Ringo Starr, Delaney and Bonnie, George Harrison, Steve Stills, Eric Clapton, and Peter Frampton.

True Love and Apple Pie

The original title of the catchy jingle and pop song *I'd Like to Teach the World to Sing* was *True Love and Apple Pie.*

Trumpet Sorrento

The first record cut by Frankie Avalon was an instrumental titled *Trumpet Sorrento.* Avalon recorded the record in 1952 as an eleven-year-old, playing lead on trumpet.

Trying To Get the Feeling Again

On the 1975 Barry Manilow album *Trying To Get the Feeling Again,* Gary Wright (later to have a huge hit with *Dream Weaver*), Alan O'Day (later to have a huge hit with *Undercover Angel*), and Melissa

Manchester (who would later have several big hit records), all sang as backup singers.

Tubular Bells

Tubular Bells is the theme music for the 1973 movie *The Exorcist,* written and performed by Mike Oldfield.

Tommy Tucker

Tommy Tucker, born Robert Higgenbotham, whose only hit record was *Hi Heel Sneakers,* was a Golden Glove boxing contender in the early 1950s.

Jethro Tull

The band Jethro Tull was named after the inventor of the seed drill.

Turn, Turn, Turn

The Byrds popularized a Pete Seeger composition when they recorded *Turn, Turn, Turn.* The words of the song were adapted by Seeger from Ecclesiastes in the Bible.

Ike Turner

Ike Turner has worked for Sam Phillips' Sun Records of Memphis as a talent scout. It was he who composed the B. B. King classic *Sweet Little Angel.*

Twelfth of Never

Johnny Mathis' 1957 ballad the *Twelfth of Never* (flip side of *Chances Are*) is based on the folk tune *The Riddle Song.*

Twins

There have been several twin combinations in rock music. In 1958 the Kalin Twins had *When* as their only hit. Charles and John Panozzo are twin members of Styx. Two members of the all-girl Shangri-Las are twins (Margie and Mary Ann Ganser), while two members of the Arbors are twin brothers (Fred and Ed Farron). Even one of the hottest groups, the Bee Gees, are blessed with twin brothers —Maurice and Robin Gibb. One can only speculate what might have happened had Elvis Presley's twin brother Jesse lived. Could the world have handled a second Elvis?

Rick Nelson and Andre Previn are both fathers of twins.

The Twist

The original version of *The Twist* was recorded by Hank Ballard and the Midnighters on King Records in 1959. However, the record company pushed the "B" side *Teardrops On Your Letter,* which soon faded. It took Ernest Evans under the pseudonym of Chubby Checker to release the almost identical version in 1960 which went on to become one of the most sold records in history.

The Twist by Chubby Checker is the only record ever to reach number one in two different years (1960 and 1962).

Dick Clark originally wanted Danny and the Juniors to record *The Twist* before Chubby Checker cut his version.

Twist and Shout

Twist and Shout, a hit song for both the Isley Brothers and the Beatles, was originally written for the Atlantic Record group the Topnotes.

Conway Twitty

Harold Jenkins changed his name to Conway Twitty by selecting two small towns on the map: Conway, Arkansas, and Twitty, Texas.

200 Motels

Ringo Starr portrayed zany singer Frank Zappa in the 1971 movie *200 Motels.*

Two Lane Blacktop

James Taylor and Dennis Wilson co-starred in the 1971 movie *Two Lane Blacktop.*

U

Upsetters

When Little Richard quit his singing career to go into the ministry, singer Dee Clark (of *Hey Little Girl* fame) took over his backup group, the Upsetters.

V

Ritchie Valens

Late singer Ritchie Valens made a rare appearance in only one movie, *Go Johnny Go* (1959).

Valentinos

It's All Over Now was originally recorded by the Valentinos, prior to the Rolling Stones release in 1964. The lead singer of the Valentinos was Bobby Womack.

Bobby Vee

On the fateful night of February 3, 1959, singers Buddy Holly, J. P. Richardson, and Ritchie Valens were killed in a Beech Bonanza en route to Fargo, North Dakota. As show business people know "the show must go on." In Fargo a local talent named Robert Velline filled in for the missing trio of superstars. Robert Velline would one day change his name to Bobby Vee, and ironically would be compared to the late Buddy Holly. Bobby Vee even recorded an album with the Crickets.

Bobby Vee once kicked Robert Zimmerman out of his band because he felt Zimmerman had no future in the music business. Zimmerman struggled along as folksinger Bob Dylan.

Vee Jay Records

Chicago's highly successful record company Vee Jay (Four Seasons, Jerry Butler, John Lee Hooker, etc.) was located on So. Michigan Boulevard just down the street from the equally successful record company Chess Records (Chuck Berry, Lee Andrews, Bo Diddley, etc.).

The Ventures

The Ventures do not perform the instrumental theme song for the television series "Hawaii Five-O," as is commonly thought. Although they did have a hit version of the song in 1969, the theme for the show was performed by Morton Stevens.

Jerry and Jim Yester

Brothers Jerry and Jim Yester had the unusual experience of both belonging to very popular rock groups. Jerry was a member of the Lovin' Spoonful while Jim sang with the Association.

The Vibrations

The group the Vibrations, who have had hits such as *The Watusi* and *My Girl Sloopy,* were originally called the Jayhawks, who had a hit in 1956 with *Stranded in the Jungle.*

Sid Vicious

Sid Vicious (real name, John Simon Ritchie) of the disbanded punk rock group the Sex Pistols was ar-

W

Adam Wade

Ballad singer Adam Wade worked with polio researcher Dr. Jonas Salk prior to becoming a professional singer.

Wake Up Little Susie

The Everly Brothers 1957 hit *Wake Up Little Susie* was "banned" in Boston.

Rick Wakeman

Clark Gable's last automobile, a blue Cadillac, was bought by Rick Wakeman in 1977.

Walk Away Renee

The Left Banke's recording of *Walk Away Renee* was based on Bach's *Pretty Ballerina.*

Walk Don't Run

The rocking instrumental *Walk Don't Run* by the Seattle group the Ventures twice made the top ten and twice sold a million copies, in 1960 and again in 1964.

The Walker Brothers

John Maus, a member of the Walker Brothers and husband of singer Kathy Young (she recorded *A Thousand Stars* in 1960), was a good friend of the Wilson Brothers in his youth and helped to teach Carl to play the guitar, prior to the Wilson Brothers becoming the Beach Boys.

Walkin' After Midnight

Prior to Patsy Cline's recording her first hit *Walkin' After Midnight* in 1957, the song was turned down by Kay Starr for whom Don Heet composed it. Patsy Cline made her television debut singing the song as a contestant on "Arthur Godfrey's Talent Scouts" in 1957.

Walking Man

If one listens carefully, the voices of Carly Simon, Peter Asher, and Paul and Linda McCartney can be heard singing the vocal backup on James Taylor's *Walking Man.*

War

Prior to becoming the successful band War, the group had previously been called Night Shift and was the backup band for Los Angeles Rams football player David Deacon Jones.

Warm Ride

Rare Earth's version of the Bee Gees' composition *Warm Ride* had the Hudson Brothers singing a typical Bee Gees harmony in the background.

Dionne Warwick

When Hal David and Burt Bacharach first discovered Dionne Warwick, she was in a studio singing backup for the Drifters, as lead singer of the Gospelaires.

Dionne Warwick once added an "e" to her name just for luck thus becoming Dionne Warwicke. Her career, for some unknown reason, took a nose dive right after.

Dionne Warwick–Mike Pinder

Dionne Warwick and Mike Pinder of the Moody Blues were both born on December 12, 1942.

Watching Scotty Grow

Bobby Goldsboro had a success in 1971 with *Watching Scotty Grow.* Many listeners believed he was singing about his own son. The truth is Scotty is the son of the song's composer Scott "Mac" Davis.

Thomas Wayne

Thomas Wayne in 1959 recorded his only hit record, titled *Tragedy*. Thomas' full name is Thomas Wayne Perkins, and he is the brother of Luther Perkins, the lead guitarist for Johnny Cash.

Thomas Wayne and Elvis Presley attended the same Memphis high school, L. C. Humes High.

We Are Not Helpless

On the Steve Stills song *We Are Not Helpless* the backing vocals were performed by such artists as:

John Sebastian, Booker T. Jones, David Crosby, Cass Elliot, Rita Coolidge, and Graham Nash.

We Five

Mike Stewart, a member of We Five, whose biggest hit *You Were On My Mind* was charted in 1966, is the brother of John Stewart, a former member of the Kingston Trio.

Bernard Webb

The composer of the 1966 Peter & Gordon hit *Woman* was credited as Bernard Webb. The composer's name was a nom de plume for Paul McCartney, who actually was the composer.

Jimmy Webb

Reverend Robert Webb, father of composer Jimmy Webb, married singer Florence LaRue, of the Fifth Dimension, to manager Marc Gordon in a hot air balloon in 1967.

Julius Wechter

Julius Wechter, founder of the unique-sounding Baja Marimba Band, was formerly a member of Martin Denny's exotic-sounding band.

The Weight

In the 1969 movie *Easy Rider,* the Band performed the song *The Weight,* yet on the sound-track album *The Weight* is performed by Smith. The reason for the replacement was the inability of two different music companies to reach an agreement.

Bob Welch

Bob Welch, ex-member of Fleetwood Mac, is the son of movie producer Robert L. Welch—*Paleface* (1948) and *Son of Paleface* (1952), both of which starred Bob Hope. His mother was an actress on radio and television.

Welcome Back Kotter

The theme song of the television series "Welcome Back Kotter" was both composed and sung by John Sebastian.

Freddy Weller

Country singer Freddy Weller was once a member of Paul Revere and the Raiders.

Cory Wells

Vocalist Cory Wells has been a member of both Paul Revere and the Raiders and, later, Three Dog Night.

Mary Wells

Mary Wells became the sister-in-law of singer Bobby Womack when she married his brother Cecil.

We've Only Just Begun

The Carpenters classic *We've Only Just Begun,* which at many weddings has replaced the traditional *I*

Love You Truly, began as a commercial for Crocker Bank in California. Paul Williams, who composed the song, was one of the members of the vocal group who sang it in the commercial.

What Am I Living For?

On April 10, 1958 Chuck Willis died after an operation in his hometown of Atlanta, Georgia. Strangely, the song he had on the charts at the time was titled *What Am I Living For?*

WHB Radio

Kansas City radio station WHB in 1955 became the first station to play *only* rock 'n' roll music.

When The Morning Comes

On Hoyt Axton's 1974 release *When the Morning Comes,* the female singing the duet with Axton is Linda Ronstadt.

What'd I Say

Ray Charles made up *What'd I Say* one evening while playing at a nightclub. He had a few minutes to kill, so he and his band extemporaneously made up the song on the spot. It became his biggest hit.

Where Did Our Love Go

The Supremes' 1964 recording of *Where Did Our Love Go* was originally planned for another Motown artist, Mary Wells.

Whipped Cream

The Tijuana Brass song *Whipped Cream* was the theme song of the television game show "The Dating Game," hosted by Jim Lange.

Barry White

At age twenty-one Barry White served as singer Jackie Lee's road manager before going into producing and eventually forming Love Unlimited.

White Rabbit

Grace Slick recorded *White Rabbit* with two rock bands, the Great Society and the Jefferson Airplane (which later became known as the Jefferson Starship).

The Jefferson Airplane's *White Rabbit* was used as the theme song for the 1973 movie *Go Ask Alice.*

Slim Whitman

Country yodeler Slim Whitman, born Otis Dewey, was a regular on the British charts during the 1950s. He became the first country artist to debut at the famed London Palladium.

The Who

The dixieland band called the Detours later changed their musical style to become the High Numbers, and then finally, The Who.

Whole Lotta Shakin' Going On

The Jerry Lee Lewis classic 1957 recording, *Whole Lotta Shakin' Going On,* his first hit record, was recorded on the first take. At first Lewis didn't want to record the song because of the suggestive lyrics, and only after Sam Phillips' persistence did he record it. John Lennon calls it the best rock song ever recorded.

Wild Child

There exist only a few recordings on which Buddy Holly played the guitar and sings but is not credited on the record. One of those recordings is the 1957 release of *Real Wild Child/Oh You Beautiful Doll* by Ivan (Jerry Allison), a member of the Crickets.

Andy Williams

Fourteen-year-old Andy Williams dubbed Lauren Bacall's singing voice in the 1944 Humphrey Bogart movie *To Have and Have Not.*

With his brothers, Andy Williams backed up Bing Crosby on the Academy Award winning song *Swinging On A Star,* from the 1944 movie *Going My Way.*

Deniece Williams

Deniece Williams, who sang duet on *Too Much, Too Little, Too Late* with Johnny Mathis (his first number-one record), was formerly a member of the female trio who sang as part of Stevie Wonder's band, Wonderlove.

Larry Williams

Singer/composer Larry Williams (four of his compositions were recorded by the Beatles) was once the valet of R & B singer Lloyd Price. Larry's first hit, *Just Because*, was previously a hit for his former employer.

Larry Williams–Carl Perkins

The Beatles have recorded four Larry Williams hits of the 1950s: *Dizzy, Miss Lizzy, Slow Down, Bad Boy* and *Lawdy Miss Clawdy.* The Fab Four also recorded three songs made popular by Carl Perkins in the 1950s: *Honey Don't, Matchbox, Everybody's Trying to Be My Baby.* (On the album *The Beatles Live! at the Starclub in Hamburg, Germany in 1962,* the Beatles sing yet another Perkins composition, *Lend Me Your Comb.*)

Mason Williams

Mason Williams, whose *Classical Gas* reached #2 on the Billboard charts in 1968, was the head writer for the "Smothers Brothers Comedy Hour" on television.

Paul Williams

Paul Williams made his movie debut as Gunther Fry in the 1965 movie *The Loved One.* He once aspired to acting prior to becoming more successful as a composer/singer.

Tony Williams

Tony Williams, for years lead singer of the extremely popular Platters, is the brother of rhythm-and-blues singer Linda Hayes.

Al Wilson

Soul artist Al Wilson was once a member of the 1950s R & B group, the Jewels, who in 1954 recorded the original version of *Hearts of Stone.*

Brian Wilson

Beach Boy member Brian Wilson once went into seclusion for a period of two years, supposedly spending much of the time in his bed.

Brian Wilson, who composes, produces, sings, and plays several instruments, is deaf in one ear. He has never heard stereo.

Dennis Wilson

Charles Manson and some of his followers were once the house guests of Beach Boy Dennis Wilson for about a year.

Hank Wilson

Hank Wilson was the pseudonym under which Leon Russell recorded country music in Nashville.

Jackie Wilson

In 1975, while performing at the Cherry Hill, New Jersey nightclub, the Latin Casino, singer Jackie Wilson experienced a stroke. To this day he is in a hospital, paralyzed.

Johnny and Edgar Winter

Brothers Johnny and Edgar Winter, both of whom had successful groups in the early 1970s, are albinos.

Edgar Winter is legally blind.

Wipe Out

In 1963 Dot Records released the album *Wipe Out* by the Surfaris. The album is one of the best instrumental stereo LPs ever recorded by a rock band, yet only two songs on the album's dozen cuts were actually recorded by the Surfaris—*Wipe Out* and *Surfer Joe*. The remaining ten songs were never credited to anyone.

Wipe Out by the Surfaris has been released on four record labels: DFS, Princess, Dot, and Decca.

Wish You Peace

The Eagles' song *I Wish You Peace* was written by Bernie Leadon and his girl friend Patti Davis. Patti Davis was a pseudonym used by Patti Reagan, the daughter of California Governor Ronald Reagan.

Peter Wolf

Rock musician Peter Wolf (leader of J. Geils Band) is married to actress Faye Dunaway, eight years his senior.

Wolfman Jack

One of the most successful DJs of all time, Wolfman Jack, who viewers first got to see in the 1973 movie *American Graffiti,* was born Robert Smith.

Stevie Wonder

Blind superartist Stevie Wonder's real name is Steveland Judkins Morris Hardaway.

In 1968 Eivets Rednow recorded an instrumental version of the song *Alfie.* Spelled backwards, the musician was actually Stevie Wonder. He also recorded an instrumental album titled *Eivets Rednow.*

Stevie Wonder has three last names: Judkins from his real father; Morris from his first stepfather; and Hardaway from his second stepfather.

In 1973 Stevie Wonder won Grammys for: Best Male Pop Vocalist; Best R&B Male Vocalist; Best R&B song (composer and for Best Album).

On August 5, 1975 Stevie Wonder signed the largest recording contract up until that time, $13 million over seven years.

The Wonder Who

The Wonder Who, an obscure group, cut two singles before they decided to reveal themselves as the highly successful Four Seasons.

Randy Wood

Two music executives of two highly successful record labels were named Randy Wood. One was the founder and president of Dot Records, while the other was the president of Vee Jay Records.

Sheb Wooley

Sheb Wooley, who in 1958 had a hit record titled *The Purple People Eater* (the song entered the pop charts in the number-one position), had been an actor for many years, appearing in numerous films, such as *High Noon* (1952). He also played Pete Nolan, the scout on the television series "Rawhide."

Sheb Wooley records comedy albums using the name Ben Colder.

On December 29, 1945, Sheb Wooley recorded the first commercial record ever in Nashville. It was recorded on the Bullet Record label.

Link Wray

In 1958 Link Wray and the Wraymen recorded a most unusual record titled *Rumble*. Link Wray has never had a hit record since, but his guitar can be heard on the number-one song of 1974, *Seasons In The Sun* by the Terry Jacks.

Betty Wright

The I.Q. level of singer Betty Wright is estimated to be in the genius range.

Y

Yardbirds

It was the up-and-coming young group the Yardbirds, who replaced the house band at Richmond's Crawdaddy Club, the Rolling Stones, when the Stones left there in 1963.

Yesterday and Today

The Beatles 1966 album *Yesterday and Today* originally showed the fab four holding parts of bloody baby dolls. Due to numerous protests, the covers were quickly replaced (in some cases new covers were pasted over the originals). These album covers are most valuable today.

You Don't Bring Me Flowers

The Barbra Streisand–Neil Diamond ballad *You Don't Bring Me Flowers* came about in a most unusual way. Both artists previously recorded the song on one of their albums. It can be found on Streisand's *Songbird* album and on Diamond's *I'm Glad You're Here with Me Tonight* album. The idea to splice together the songs was that of WAKY disc jockey Gary Guthrie. Subsequently, the two artists combined their talents on the song, and a hit was born.

You Don't Bring Me Flowers has become Columbia Record's best-selling record in their ninety-three-year history.

Neil Diamond changed the name of the album *You Don't Bring Me Flowers* from its original title *The American Popular Song* because of the popularity of the duet with Barbra Streisand.

Bob Gaudio, an ex-member of Frankie Valli's Four Seasons, produced *You Don't Bring Me Flowers.*

You Talk Too Much

Joe Jones' 1960 top-ten hit *You Talk Too Much* was actually recorded by Jones on three different occasions on four different record labels before it became a seller. In 1954 he first recorded it on Capitol, where it didn't do anything. Then in 1957 Herald Records released a version by Jones, but again it went nowhere. Finally in 1960 Joe Jones recorded it a third time on the New Orleans Ric label which was bought up and released on the Roulette label, and an "overnight" hit was born.

Young Love

Young Love twice topped the British charts, first in 1957 when actor Tab Hunter made a version, and then sixteen years later in 1973 when Donny Osmond recut the song.

The Young Rascals

Prior to becoming a member of the Young Rascals, Gene Cornish recorded *I Want To Be A Beatle* as Gene Cornish and the Unbeatables.

The Youngbloods

The Youngbloods provided the music for the 1970–1971 TV series "Hot Dog."

Your Mama Don't Dance

Loggins and Messina's classic rocker *Your Mama Don't Dance* is actually based on the Rooftop Singers' 1963 song, *Mama Don't Allow*.

You're So Fine

The 1959 Falcons' hit record *You're So Fine* featured artists Eddie Floyd and Joe Stubbs, brother of the Four Tops lead singer Levi Stubbs. In 1961 Wilson Picket became a member of the group.

You're So Vain

Supposedly, the person Carly Simon had in mind when she sang *You're So Vain* was actor Warren Beatty, with whom she had once been associated. Mick Jagger was one of the singers in the vocal background of the song.

You're The One

The Vogues' first hit song, *You're The One* (1965), was written by Petula Clark.

Z

Michael Zager

Michael Zager and Barry Manilow were fellow employees in the CBS television mailroom in Los Angeles.

Frank Zappa—Don Van Vliet

Frank Zappa and Don Van Vliet (AKA Captain Beefheart) both attended the same Antelope Valley High School in Glendale, California, in the 1960s. It was Zappa who nicknamed Don "Captain Beefheart."

Zapple

Zapple Records was the only subsidiary label of the Beatles' Apple Records.

Warren Zevon

Warren Zevon was once a member and director of the band that backed the Everly Brothers.

Zip-A-Dee-Doo-Dah

Leon Russell, Glen Campbell, Nino Tempo, and Billy Strange were all session musicians on the Bob B. Soxx and the Blue Jeans hit record *Zip-A-Dee-Doo-Dah,* a Phil Spector production.

The Zombies

The Zombies performed three songs in the 1965 Otto Preminger movie, *Bunny Lake Is Missing*.

The End

Earl Grant, the Doors, the Beatles, and Nico have all recorded songs titled *The End*.

And that's thirty ....

Dedicated to the Memory of . . .

1954	Johnny Ace	(1929–1954)	Shot Himself
1958	Chuck Willis	(1928–1958)	Illness After Surgery
1959	Buddy Holly	(1936–1959)	Plane Crash
	Ritchie Valens	(1941–1959)	Plane Crash
	J. P. Richardson	(1935–1959)	Plane Crash
	Guitar Slim	(1926–1959)	Cancer
1960	Eddie Cochran	(1938–1960)	Automobile Accident
	Johnny Horton	(1927–1960)	Automobile Accident
	Jesse Belvin	(1933–1960)	Automobile Accident
1963	Patsy Cline	(1932–1963)	Plane Crash
	Dinah Washington	(1924–1963)	Drug Poisoning
1964	Sam Cooke	(1935–1964)	Gunshot
	Jim Reeves	(1924–1964)	Plane Crash
	Johnny Burnette	(1934–1964)	Drowned
1965	Nat "King" Cole	(1919–1965)	Cancer
	Alan Freed	(1922–1965)	Uremia

1966	Bobby Fuller	(1943–1966)	Asphyxiation
	Richard Farina	(1937–1966)	Motorcycle Accident
1967	Otis Redding	(1941–1967)	Plane Crash
	Woody Guthrie	(1912–1967)	Huntington's Chorea
1968	Frankie Lymon	(1942–1968)	Overdose
	Little Willie John	(1937–1968)	Pneumonia
1969	Brian Jones	(1944–1969)	Drowned
	Roy Hamilton	(1929–1969)	Stroke
1970	Earl Grant	(1931–1970)	Automobile Accident
	Jimi Hendrix	(1942–1970)	Overdose
	Janis Joplin	(1943–1970)	Overdose
	Alan Wilson (Canned Heat)	(1943–1970)	Drug Poisoning
	Tammi Terrell	(1946–1970)	Brain Damage
	Billy Stewart	(1938–1970)	Automobile Accident
Slim Harpo		(1924–1970)	Heart Attack

1971	King Curtis	(1934–1971)	Murdered
	Jim Morrison	(1944–1971)	Heart Attack
	Junior Parker	(1932–1971)	Brain Tumor
	Gene Vincent	(1935–1971)	Hemorrhage
	Donald McPherson	(1941–1971)	Leukemia
	Duane Allman	(1946–1971)	Motorcycle Accident
1972	Clyde Mcphatter	(1931–1972)	Heart Attack
	Danny Whitten	(–1972)	Overdose
	Berry Oakley	(1948–1972)	Motorcycle Accident
	Les Harvey	(–1972)	Electrocuted
1973	Jim Croce	(1943–1973)	Plane Crash
	Bobby Darin	(1936–1973)	Heart Problem
	Gram Parsons	(1946–1973)	Overdose
	Clarence White (Byrds)	(1944–1973)	Stomach Hemorrhage
	Ron (Pigpen) Mc-Kernan	(1945–1973)	Suicide

	Paul Williams (Temptations)	(1939–1973)	Suicide
1974	Mama Cass	(1943–1974)	Choked to Death
	Robbie Mc-Intosh	(1944–1974)	Overdose
	Ivory Joe Hunter	(1911–1974)	Lung Cancer
	Nick Drake	(–1974)	Overdose
	Arthur "Big Boy" Crudup	(1905–1974)	Stroke
1975	Al Jackson	(1935–1975)	Shot by a Burglar
	Pete Ham (Badfinger)	(1947–1975)	Suicide
	Tim Buckley	(1947–1975)	Overdose
	Tommy Bolin	(–1975)	Overdose
1976	Sal Mineo	(1939–1976)	Murdered
	Phil Reed	(–1976)	Fell from Hotel Window
	Phil Ochs	(1940–1976)	Suicide
	Howlin' Wolf (Chester Burnett)	(1910–1976)	Cancer

Year	Name	Dates	Cause
	Paul Kossoff	(–1976)	Heart Trouble
	Freddie King	(1934–1976)	Ulcers
	Chris Kenner	(–1976)	Heart Attack
	Florence Ballard	(1943–1976)	Heart Attack
1977	Elvis Presley	(1935–1977)	Heart Attack (Controversial)
	Ronnie Van Zant	(1949–1977)	Plane Crash
	Steve Gaines	(–1977)	Plane Crash
	Marc Bolan	(1948–1977)	Automobile Accident
1978	Terry Kath	(1946–1978)	Self-Inflicted Gunshot
	Sandy Denny	(1947–1978)	Fall at Home
	Gregory Herbert (Blood, Sweat and Tears)	(–1978)	Overdose
1979	Donny Hathaway	(1945–1979)	Suicide
	Sid Vicious	(1958–1979)	Overdose
	Van McCoy	(1941–1979)	Heart Attack

Minnie Riperton	(1948–1979)	Cancer
Lowell George	(1945–1979)	Heart Attack
Dorsey Burnette	(1932–1979)	Heart Attack

And to so many more great people who gave their lives to that music which has brought so much enjoyment into our lives.

FUN & GAMES FROM WARNER BOOKS

BAR GAMES BETS AND CHALLENGES
by Alan Ericksen *(V90-648, $1.95)*
Here are all the basic rules, preliminaries, descriptions of play, psychology of play and tips on barroom games using coins or paper money, matches, swizzle sticks, coasters, and even olives. Ericksen shows how to figure the probabilities and odds as well as do all the tricks.

THE AMAZIN' BILL MAZER'S BASEBALL TRIVIA BOOK
by Bill Mazer and Stan Fischler *(S91-784, $2.50)*
Bill Mazer is the sportscaster that nobody can beat. Now he makes you an expert too. The record makers and breakers; blasts from baseball's past; game anecdotes and player stories you won't want to miss; and little-known facts and figures. Bill Mazer has the facts and gives them to you in amusing anecdotes, quickie quizzes, and question and answer stumpers.

BARTENDER'S GUIDE TO BASEBALL
by Dick Lally *(S91-736, $2.50)*
Forty challenging quizzes containing over 2000 questions and answers, this book covers the whole range of baseball under short subject areas. Pitching, hitting, World Series, Hall of Fame, rookies, All Star Game MVP and even a section on baseball movies.

HIGH & INSIDE
The Complete Guide to Baseball Slang
by Joseph McBride *(S91-939, $2.50)*
This book answers the question "Why do they call it . . .?" for over 1000 baseball terms and nicknames. Loaded with definitions and origins plus a dictionary of nicknames with the background of each. And baseball one-liners that have been quoted often with their courses and stories.